# GLIMPSES OF
# HIS GLORY

## A Revelation of God's Character
## Through His Names and Titles

"I am the Lord [YHWH], that is My name; and My glory I will not give to another, nor My praise to carved images."

–Isaiah 42:8

# GLIMPSES OF
# HIS GLORY

## A Revelation of God's Character
## Through His Names and Titles

### Yvonne Shelton

**MHP**

MAGNIFY HIM
PUBLISHING

# GLIMPSES OF
# HIS GLORY

Content Editing: Yvonne Shelton, Ruth Stewart

Cover Design: Ricky Carter
Cover Photo: GettyImages.com
Text Design: Greg Solie • Altamont Graphics

ISBN: 978-0-9664314-1-4

# Table of Contents

"And they who know Your name will lean on and confidently put their trust in You, for You, Lord, have not forsaken those who seek You."

—Psalm 9:10 AMPC

# Preface

I never planned to write this book. In fact, I had been working on another book when the inspiration came to write this one. You see, I was reading a book about re-kindling one's prayer life (I felt my prayer life needed bolstering) when I came across the suggestion that a study into the names and titles of God had made such a difference for the author.

I have always had a fascination with names. In fact, I will invariably ask someone who is recounting the birth of a new family member or friend, "What is his/her name?" It somehow helps me to make a connection with the person in the story. It is no surprise to me that I would be consumed with the desire to study the names and titles of God.

I cannot say when I felt impressed to write Glimpses of His Glory, but the format took shape as the Holy Spirit impressed me to share some of these insights. First of all, I could not even pronounce some of these names, so a proper pronunciation was necessary. I called one of my Jewish friends, Kenny Karen, and consulted with him on the correct pronunciations. Kenny is a secular Jew and although this was not his current focus, as the son of an Orthodox rabbi he had studied Hebrew and coached me on the proper way to pronounce the names and titles.

I needed some assistance with some of the Hebrew concepts, such as using YHWH vs. Jehovah. I had to get some deeper insights so I contacted my friend and co-3ABN Board member, Dr. Carmelita Troy. She is a faculty member at Andrews University. I asked her to introduce me to a Hebrew scholar there at Andrews who could assist me. She connected me with Dr. Roy Gane, Professor of Hebrew Bible and Ancient Near Eastern Languages at Andrews. He answered my questions, gave me the phonetic spellings of the names and titles of God in these chapters, and shared the information that is included in the appendix.

Then, I felt impressed to share a verse from the Bible that introduced each of the names of God to the reader. That idea came about as I was talking to Dwight Hall, CEO of Remnant Publications, and a contributor to one of the chapters. As I was giving him the concept of the book and what it would include, he suggested that I add the biblical context for the name. That also crystalized for me the idea of having the scripture and the context as an introduction to a story that is a modern demonstration of the attribute.

I have interviewed many people on 3ABN whose testimonies are jaw dropping. I have heard these stories from former drug dealers, a hit man from a drug cartel, a former Muslim who was stoned for his conversion to Christ, etc. Their victories over seemingly insurmountable obstacles fit right into this concept of God's great exploits in their lives. I contacted the contributors for each story in this book and they allowed me to share a bit of their journey with you. I know that you will be as blessed as I was as you read how God intervened in their lives, and it will remind you of His goodness in your own life.

Finally, at each chapter's end, there is a prayer that I encourage you to pray aloud to God. I decided to include this as a practical application of the featured name. Several years ago, I was going through a painful situation, and I read a book that included a prayer at the end of each chapter. Praying it aloud to God really made a difference in my response to the challenge that I was facing at the time. I pray that it will make a difference in your response as well.

Blessings, as you read and receive *Glimpses of His Glory.*

Yvonne Shelton
July 26, 2020

# Introduction

What is in a name? In modern times names are given for identification purposes, but in ancient times names had a different significance. At birth, the name given to a child actually forecast the character and life direction of the child. The parents, when ascribing a name to their child, were assigning a purpose and direction in their training.

Great honor or dishonor was attached to a name. The name displayed the character-focus of the life of the child. For example, Jesus (Yeshua) was given that name because He would "save His people from their sins" (Matthew 1:21).

In media and popular culture, Satan seeks to distort the character and personality of God. It is my desire to exalt and magnify our great God through the exposure to some of His names and titles. This book will not be an exhaustive study of the names of God, but rather an introduction to many of them with emphasis on how they apply to our daily situations.

This is a book of testimonies— stories of men and women whose lives have been forever changed by the intervention of an awesome, compassionate God. His attributes do not work independently of each other but are complementary, reflecting His character and personality. All manifest His essential nature of love.

In Bible days, people thought that knowing God's name would offer unique access to Him, and that those who had this knowledge had a kind of spiritual power and advantage. It opened the door to a deeper understanding of His character and personality. That is the purpose of this book. The intent is to move you, the reader, toward a deeper connection with God through His names and titles.

**YHWH: The Sacred, Unutterable Name of God**
(Pronunciation unknown, but probably something like "Yahweh" and
derived from the verb "to be"; the personal name of Israel's deity)

*"I appeared to Abraham, to Isaac, and to Jacob, as
God Almighty [El Shaddai], but by My name* LORD
*[YHWH] I was not known to them." (Exodus 6:3)*

About midway in writing this book, I hit a wall. I had quite a time deciding which name was the correct name to use: Yahweh, or Jehovah. I wanted to be as authentic with the early Hebrew as possible and not to lead anyone to use an incorrect name. That would be a catastrophe: to lead people to the WRONG name of our God. I pled with the Lord to show me the correct name to use.

After much prayer, and consulting with Dr. Roy Gane, I felt led to use YHWH, which is an English transliteration of the Hebrew Tetragrammaton (four letters) designated as God's personal name. For all the "academics" out there, if you want a deeper explanation into the etymology of Yahweh and Jehovah, please read the appendix at the back of this book.

His **written** name here is transliterated as YHWH, but since no one knows for sure how to pronounce it, His **spoken** titles, in place of YHWH will be El, Adonai, or, the LORD (all uppercase letters). Please note that in many cases, the Names of God Bible (God's Word Translation) is used as the chapter's foundational text as it contains the Hebrew names and titles of God.

Each chapter in *Glimpses of His Glory* contains the proper pronunciation (written phonetically) of the name or title, a text in which that name is found, a biblical context for the name, a story that demonstrates God's amazing intervention, and ends with a prayer that you can read out loud to Him. The testimonies in this book have truly blessed me. I pray that you too will find new insight into the character and love of our great God and King.

# – Chapter 1 –
# Elohim:
# God
## (Ehl-oh-heem)

*"In the beginning Elohim created heaven*
*and earth." (Genesis 1:1 NOG)*

The very first verse of the Bible introduces us to *Elohim: Mighty God.* [1] It is the first name that God uses to announce Himself to us. Elohim is used 2,570 times in the Scriptures. There are several points of interest regarding the title Elohim. First of all, it is a plural noun, yet followed by a singular verb, or described by a singular adjective. Andrew Jukes explains it like this: "The plural form of the first name of God, that is, 'Elohim,' shadows forth the same mystery; while the verb, and even the adjective, joined with it in the singular, as when we read, 'the living,' or 'the righteous,' or 'the Most High God,' shew that this 'Elohim,' though plural, is but One God." [2]

Our Creator God, from the outset, gave us a glimpse of His glory by demonstrating both His plurality (as in the Trinity) and His "Oneness." Elohim represents the Godhead: Father, Son, and Holy Spirit. All three were present at creation, and all three are in covenant relationship with one another which brings us to another interesting point about the name Elohim.

Elohim describes One Who stands in covenant relationship ratified by an oath. Within the Godhead there is a covenant bond. "For this covenant relationship, which the name 'Elohim' expresses, is first a relationship in God. He is One, but in Him also, as His name declares, there is plurality; and in this plurality, He has individual relationships, both in and with Himself, which, because He is God, can never be dissolved or broken. [3] Thus, as Parkhurst says, this name contains the mystery of the Trinity." [4] There are some interesting parallels between God's original acts of creation, and how He re-creates us. In Genesis 1:3, Elohim begins by saying, *"Let there be light."* And the Bible says in Genesis 1:4 that He *"divided the light from the darkness.*" It is in this same way that Elohim begins our re-creation into His image. He shines His light into our darkened lives, and we are convicted of our sinfulness. He separates the light from the darkness in our hearts.

Through the power of His Spirit, we begin to recognize sin for what it truly is. He teaches us how to be victorious in Him as we respond to the light, His light, and distance ourselves (through His power) from the dominion of sin.

On the second day of Creation, Elohim created the sky. Jeremiah 10:12 says He *"has stretched out the heavens at His discretion."* And so it is in our lives. Elohim stretches us in new directions as we come to Him. We begin the disciplines of Bible study, prayer, and acknowledgment of Him and His working in our lives.

On the third day of Creation, Elohim made the fruits and vegetables. Again, there is a parallel in our spiritual growth experience. As we get to know our Savior, Jesus (Yeshua), we begin to grow and bear the fruits of the Spirit: love, joy, peace, patience, kindness, goodness, faithfulness, gentleness, and self-control (see Galatians 5: 22–23).

On the fourth day, Elohim created the sun, moon, and stars. In Genesis 1:14–15 He said:

> "'Let there be lights in the firmament of the heavens to divide the day from the night; and let them be for signs and seasons, and for days and years; and let them be for lights in the firmament of the heavens to give light on the earth'; and it was so."

In our broken lives, Elohim gives us His Holy Spirit and His Word (the Bible) to be the lights that lead us out of spiritual darkness. His Spirit rules in our hearts, and His Word is a *"lamp unto my feet, and a light unto my path"* (Psalm 119:105).

The fifth day was the day in which Elohim created living creatures: birds, fish, and animals. He brought forth LIFE. That is what He does for us. He gives us new life in Him. Second Corinthians 5:17 says, *"Therefore, if anyone is in Christ, he is a new creation; old things have passed away; behold, all things have become new."*

Only Elohim can create life, and only He can make us new in Him. He is our Creator and Sustainer. Andrew Jukes has a beautiful quote about Elohim. He said, "And by His work in us He makes us know what it is to have a covenant-God, whose fullness meets our every want, and whose very name and nature is the pledge of our deliverance." [5] On the sixth day, Elohim created man and woman. He said:

> *"Let Us make man in Our image, according to Our likeness; let them have dominion over the fish of the sea, over the birds of the air, and over the cattle, over all the earth, and over every creeping thing that creeps on the earth...Then God saw everything that He had made, and indeed it was very good. So the evening and the morning were the sixth day." (Genesis 1:26, 31)*

God shaped and formed man from the dust of the ground. And so it is with us. Elohim shapes and creates our inner man to conform to the image of Christ.

The work of creation ended on the seventh day:

> *"And on the seventh day God ended His work which He had done...Then God blessed the seventh day and sanctified it, because in it He rested from all His work which God had created and made." (Genesis 2:2–3)*

Creation was complete. Elohim "blessed and sanctified the seventh day." That means that the seventh day establishes Elohim as the Creator God and has been set apart by Him for a holy purpose (sanctified). It is a day of spiritual rejuvenation and growth.

And so it is with us. The process of sanctification is the work of a lifetime in us. It will be the completion of Elohim's re-creative process. He continues to shape and grow us until His return to take us home to be with Him. Only God can sanctify us and set us apart for a holy purpose.

Glory be to Elohim, the Mighty Creator God. He is in the business of Regeneration, Re-creation, and Restoration.

Chris had a lot of darkness in his life. He did not know that Elohim had a plan:

## Chris's Story

At the age of 19, Chris decided to go into the entertainment industry. He wrote "treatments" for music videos. Treatments are the storyline for a video (what is going to happen in the video, the flow of it, etc.). Later, he was offered the opportunity to write a movie script. He was called into his manager's office and told that there was a movie script needed. "When do you need it?" he asked. "By 8 p.m. tomorrow," his manager said. "Tomorrow night?" Chris thought this could be his major shot at success.

He went to a store and bought a can of coffee. He wrote and wrote. When he became tired, he dug into the coffee can and ATE three to four handfuls of the coffee. By 8 p.m. the next night, Chris dropped off a 200+ page movie script at his manager's office. From there, he got other projects (movies and pilots). The average manuscript takes at least six months to write. Chris was doing it in under two weeks.

Chris wrote most of his scripts at his girlfriend's house. She was a Haitian, and her father practiced voodoo in the house. Chris smoked and sold marijuana at the time and would get high over there. One day, Chris went home from their house and looked in the mirror. He saw something in his eyes that wasn't him, and he smiled. He knew that the entity looking back at him was helping him write the scripts and experience success in the industry. By this time, he was writing screenplays, making money, and hanging out with the entertainment industry's top performers.

One day, the Lord spoke into Chris's spirit. He told him to stop what he was doing, stop smoking marijuana and go back to school to become a preacher. That very night, Chris told one of his buddies that he was leaving the industry. The friend could not believe it. What was Chris thinking? He was so successful. Why leave it all now? Over the next few weeks, several of Chris's friends heard about his upcoming departure, and many of them accepted the Lord because of his witness.

Chris left the industry and went to a school where he would receive training to become a minister. Unfortunately, according to Chris, his conversion was incomplete. He had not totally surrendered his life to Christ. The very first week at the school Chris looked around at the students carrying their books, going to classes, and asked himself, "What am I doing here? These kids are all studying to have a career and get jobs. I already had a good one." So he packed up and went back to New York.

Chris got right back into the game. Only this time, he could not write anything. He made several attempts to write but nothing would come. He felt that God was blocking him, and the only way to change that was to denounce Him. Chris went to a jewelry store and purchased some rosary beads. He knew that they had a pagan origin. Then, he ordered an upside-down cross indicating his rejection of Christ's atonement for his sins. Chris bought some weed (marijuana), turned on some hip-hop music, and let it play over and over again. He kept looking in the mirror, and in time he saw the old look that he had had before. Then, it all came back to him. The entity that was "helping" him was back. He finished the project.

After completing the project, Chris wanted to take a trip to the Bahamas. One day, he booked a 10:00 p.m. flight. Around mid-afternoon of that very day, he went shopping for his journey. While heading to the store, he spotted some guys in the neighborhood who sold weed. He stopped and bought a dime bag ($10.00) and continued to the store.

While in the store, two undercover detectives cornered him and arrested him. During all of the times that Chris had sold weed, he had never been arrested. Now, having only a small amount on him and not being a dealer, he got nailed. "God is doing this," Chris thought. He put it out of his mind. His next thought was, "If I can go to night court, I can still make my flight."

During the booking process, while others who had been arrested were making noise and being unruly, Chris was silent. He knew that God was stopping him. The detectives had watched him throughout the entire process and knew that there was something different about him.

When arrested, Chris had over $2,000 on his person. Typically, whatever is found on the person who is arrested is used as evidence and having over $2,000 is indicative that the person is a distributor or drug dealer. The detectives had confiscated the money upon his arrest. After observing Chris, one of the detectives quietly handed him the money back and said, "Put this in your sock, under your foot." God, in His mercy, was showing Chris that He was with him through all of this. Elohim was not finished with him. But He still did not have Chris's total attention.

Chris went to court but missed his flight that night. He left the court furious. "Why doesn't God just leave me alone?" He was not out of court for two hours before he found himself in a hospital fighting for his life. Chris's fury with God led him into an altercation with someone, which in turn, led to injuries that caused him to be hospitalized. His right arm was severely cut. Chris almost bled out. It became clear to him that his new direction would lead to death. He needed to make a decision. It was at that point that he decided to return to Jesus and to give his heart to him. But Elohim was not finished with him yet.

Chris started going back to church, studying the Word, and sharing his faith whenever the opportunity presented itself. He began to have a day-to-day relationship with Jesus and was getting to know Him better. He knew that God had a plan for his life, but he did not know what it was, and this frustrated him. The pain from Chris's injuries was very severe. It was so intense that he had to take pain medicine. It was opioids, and Chris became addicted to them.

It got to the point where Chris found himself just trying to get more of the drugs. He remembers going to a young doctor who told him, "Don't worry about it. I'll give you anything that you want." This doctor *increased* Chris's dosage. Again, Satan was trying to destroy a life that was broken, but Elohim was not finished with Chris.

The next time he went to see the doctor, the young one was not there. This time, an older, caring physician talked to him and really examined him. He asked Chris how long he had worn the cast, and was dismayed when he found out that it had been on for such a long time (a few months) without any physical therapy. He cut off the cast and told Chris that he was to begin treatment on that hand and arm immediately, or he was going to lose its usage. Chris was horrified. He did not want to lose his hand.

He went home and fell before God, the Supreme God of the universe, Elohim, and begged Him to tell him what He wanted him to do with his life. Chris asked for a sign, a dream, something that would allow him to know what God expected of him.

That night, the Lord gave Chris a dream. He dreamed that he was in the middle of New York City, in Manhattan. The street that he was on was extra wide with multiple lanes. Cars were scurrying, and there was a filthy crosswalk. Right by the crosswalk, Chris saw a bucket with a scrub brush. He picked up the brush and began to wash the filthy crosswalk. He would stay in one area until it was clean, then move on to the next, systematically cleaning the crosswalk so that its path became clear.

Two guys in black watched him and said to him, "You are cleaning the crosswalk?" Chris answered, "Well, somebody's got to do it." In the dream, Chris's arm was moving back and forth as he cleaned the crosswalk. He must have been pushing it in his sleep because his arm hit the wall, and he woke up in excruciating pain. The dream was so real.

Two days later, as he contemplated that dream, he laughed to himself about how he had hit his hand against the wall and awakened himself as he was "cleaning" the crosswalk. The Lord spoke to his heart and said, "Don't laugh. This was a serious dream." He went on to tell Chris that the street was a symbol of the world: fast-paced and dangerous. The crosswalk represented the way to eternal life: the narrow gate. Matthew 7:13–14 says:

*"Enter by the narrow gate; for wide is the gate and broad is the way that leads to destruction, and there are many who go in by it. Because narrow is the gate and difficult is the way which leads to life, and there are few who find it."*

The two guys in black represented those who, along the way, would try to discourage Chris from his mission.

Some people want to get through life, but if they cannot see the correct path, how will they know the Way? The Lord told Chris, "You must make the path straight for them." It was the John the Baptist message. That is how the name, the "Forerunner," came to be. Since that dream, Chris, the Forerunner, who has a large internet following (praise God), has been on a mission to make the path straight for those who are seeking God. Chris is now very intentional concerning his walk with the Lord. He knows that Elohim is not finished with him or any of us yet.

## Prayer:

*"**Elohim, Mighty God, and Creator**, I honor You. You are the Creator of all life. But, most importantly, You offer me a new life in You. As my Creator, You are continuously re-creating me— my appetites, desires, and pursuits. Conform me to the image of Your Son, my Lord and Savior Jesus Christ (Yeshua). Sanctify me by Your Spirit and strengthen my areas of weakness. In my heart, shine Your marvelous light into my brokenness.*

*"Then, just as You stretched out the heavens, stretch me in my spiritual disciplines such as prayer and Bible study. Help my life to be fruitful and help me to witness for You. Give me Your Holy Spirit to separate the light from the darkness and convict me of my sinfulness. Give me Your Word to keep me on the right*

*path. In Christ, I have a new life. Conform me to His image and set me apart for Your holy purpose. Create in me a clean heart, oh Elohim."*

# – Chapter 2 –
# Go'el:
# God My Redeemer, Deliverer
## (go-ehl)

*"They turned from their sins and eagerly looked for
El. They remembered that Elohim was their rock, that
El Elyon was their Go'el." (Psalm 78:34–35 NOG)*

Go'el means "Redeemer, Deliverer." [6] The title *Go'el* is first seen in the book of Job. Let's take a look at Job for a few minutes. He was an incredibly wealthy man and is said to have been the most influential person in the Middle East in his time.

Job had integrity and a deep relationship with God. His connection with God was so strong that Satan challenged God by saying that Job only served Him because of all the blessings. Remove the benefits, Satan said, and Job would curse God. So YHWH told Satan, *"Everything he has is in your power, but you must not lay a hand on him!"* (Job 1:12 NOG) [7]

Satan destroyed Job's livestock, killed his children, and massacred his servants. Despite all of that, Job praised the name of YHWH. Satan went back to God and re-challenged Him by getting permission to afflict Job himself. The Lord told Satan, "He is in your power, but you must save his life." So Satan struck Job with painful, itchy boils from the soles of his feet to the crown of his head. Job, although he was confused about why all of this had happened to him, was resolute in his trust in God.

Job knew that YHWH would one day vindicate him of any perceived wrong-doing. Job needed someone to deliver him from this scourge. Who would rescue him from this curse? In Job 19:25 (NOG), he said, *"I know that my Go'el lives, and afterwards, he will rise on the earth."*

In spite of all that he had been through, Job had enough faith in his Go'el to know that He had always been there for him in the past, would continue to do so in the future, and one day he would see Him face to face. Job refused to disparage his God, and Job was redeemed.

God blessed the latter end of Job's life more than the beginning. He restored Job's wealth, his reputation, and gave him ten more children.

Job died having had a long, full life. YHWH was Job's redeemer. His trust in his Go'el was resolute and ultimately rewarded.

The second book of the Bible that mentions go'el is the book of Ruth. Here, this Hebrew word appears thirteen times.[8] The go'el was the kinsman-redeemer alluded to in Leviticus.[9] In early Bible times, society depended upon the kinsman-redeemer to avenge any wrong done to a family member. The kinsman-redeemer would also buy the freedom of the slave, or marry the widow of a close relative to ensure the survival of the bloodline of the deceased husband. This would deliver the widow from destitution.

Ruth was an immigrant in Israel. She was a widow, originally from Moab, and along with her widowed mother-in-law, Naomi, had decided to leave Moab and go to Naomi's homeland, Bethlehem. Ruth and Naomi were dedicated to one another. Ruth cared for her mother-in-law as best she could, but both of them were women in a society in which women without husbands were often in poverty.

One of the worst financial positions that a woman could be in was widowhood. In Israel, in Bible times, it was the duty of the closest male relative of any unattached woman to marry her and care for her. Boaz was a close living relative of Naomi's late husband, Elimelech. Boaz was wealthy and had observed Ruth harvesting from his fields. He saw her integrity and compassion and knew her reputation for the love and care of Naomi.

Boaz was an astute businessman and well respected by his workers and community. When he realized that he was a kinsman-redeemer for Ruth (because of Naomi), he also knew that there was a closer male relative who was next in line. He told Ruth that if the family member would not marry her, then he, Boaz, would.

Boaz did not let any grass grow under his feet. He went into town and met with the kinsman who was the closest relative of Naomi's husband. He reminded him of Naomi's return from Moab and told him that she was selling the land that belonged to Elimelech.

The offer was made to the kinsman to purchase the property. He agreed to do so. When Boaz explained that the family member would also need to marry Ruth so that she could bear children who would carry on the husband's name and keep their land in the family, the family kinsman refused to do it, saying that it might endanger his own estate. He told Boaz to buy the property.

Boaz, upon making sure that the transaction was witnessed and completed, declared that he would marry Ruth. He rescued Ruth and

Naomi from lives of poverty and loneliness. Boaz was Ruth's hero, her kinsman-redeemer, her go'el.

It is exciting that when the title *Go'el* is applied to God, we get a glimpse of the gospel itself. There are several parallels between the concept of the Go'el in the Old Testament, and the work of Yeshua (Jesus). [10] First of all, the Go'el must be *related by blood* to those whom He redeems (emphasis added). [11] Jesus has redeemed us to God by His blood:

> *"You are worthy to take the scroll, and to open its seals;*
> *for you were slain. And have redeemed us to God by*
> *Your blood out of every tribe and tongue and people*
> *and nation." (Revelation 5:9)*

It is the blood of Jesus that covers every sin that we have ever committed and could even possibly commit. Our sins are covered because Jesus' blood is sufficient. His blood has redeemed us and set us free from the control and power of the enemy, Satan.

Secondly, the Go'el must be able to pay the price for redemption: [12]

> *"Inasmuch then as the children have partaken of flesh and blood,*
> *He Himself likewise shared in the same, that through death He*
> *might destroy him who had the power of death, that is, the devil,*
> *and release those who through fear of death were all their lifetime*
> *subject to bondage....Therefore, in all things He had to be made*
> *like His brethren, that He might be a merciful and faithful High*
> *Priest in things pertaining to God, to make propitiation for the*
> *sins of the people." (Hebrews 2:14–15, 17)*

> *"Knowing that you were not redeemed with corruptible things like*
> *silver or gold, from your aimless conduct received by tradition*
> *from your fathers, but with the precious blood of Christ, as of a*
> *lamb without blemish and without spot." (1 Peter 1:18–19)*

Thirdly, the Go'el must be willing to redeem: [13]

> *"Just as the Son of Man did not come to be served, but to serve,*
> *and to give His life a ransom for many." (Matthew 20:28)*

*"As the Father knows Me, even so I know the Father, and I lay down My life for the sheep....No one takes it from Me, but I lay it down of Myself. I have the power to lay it down, and I have power to take it again. This command I have received from My Father."* (John 10:15,18)

Finally, the Go'el must be free himself. [14] Christ was free from sin:

*"For He made Him who knew no sin to be sin for us, that we might become the righteousness of God in Him." (2 Corinthians 5:21)*

*"For to this you were called, because Christ also suffered for us, leaving us an example, that you should follow His steps: 'Who committed no sin, nor was deceit found in His mouth.'"* (1 Peter 2:21–22)

Jesus (Yeshua) is our Redeemer, our Go'el. From the foundation of the world, it was determined that He would pay the price for our sins and redeem us from its bondage. He shed His own blood to reconcile us to God. Everyone who believes in Him has been rescued from the slavery of sin. Our Go'el, Yeshua, has paid the ransom for us so that we might be free.

## Vala's Story

From a very early age, Vala felt unloved and unwanted by her mother. Her mother, at 13, had married Vala's father, a much older man, and had always resented him. She wanted to get away from him. When Vala was around seven years old, her mother stopped by her school to see her. Vala felt that something was going on. Later, she realized that her mother had come to say goodbye.

Vala did not see her again for another six years. She asked various relatives about her mother, but no one would tell her where she went. After a while, she found out that her mom had escaped to Sweden. Around the same time that her mother left, her father joined the Peshmerga (a Kurdish group that was fighting the Iraqi government). She basically lost both parents at the same time.

During her early years, Vala's life was chaotic. She bounced back and forth between her paternal and maternal relatives. No one really wanted her except her maternal grandmother and her mother's younger brother, Samuel. Her maternal grandfather wanted to kick her out of the house because he was angry at Vala's mother for leaving her husband. They came from a Muslim household where the man rules and shame concerns are often significant. Vala's mother had disgraced the family by leaving her husband.

Vala's father's relatives would call her names and say that they could not stand to look at her because she reminded them of her mother. At age eight or nine was the first time that Vala considered suicide. Her heart was so heavy from the multiple rejections. She considered jumping off her grandmother's roof, but when she got up on it, it looked too scary. Then she thought about taking her grandmother's medications. She could not bring herself to do it at that point.

Vala's paternal relatives were devout Muslims, so she too started to pray to Allah as they did, but she was not comforted. Following her family's spiritual path just did not seem to work for her.

When Vala was ten years old, her father returned from the war and for a brief time she felt some happiness. Vala felt close to her father. Her joy was short-lived, however, and by the time she was 11, the pain became unbearable: no love (except from her father, uncle Samuel, and maternal grandmother), failure at school, etc. Suicide, Vala thought, would just make everyone's life easier, so she decided to try again.

This time, she took an overdose of all the medicines that her grandmother had. Vala ended up in the hospital. She did not die. She was miserable and in despair. She sank into a deeper depression. Vala's only joy was when her maternal grandmother would go and get her and bring her over to their home. They were not as religious as Vala's father's relatives, so she had more freedom to play with the neighborhood kids.

One day, when she was 13, she found out that she could go and live with her mother in Sweden. Her grandfather and uncle Samuel were going to leave Iraq and reunite with her mother there. Vala was full of hope. She was going to see her beloved mother again! All of those years of separation were behind her, and she would have a new beginning with her mother.

Things did not turn out as Vala had planned. For one thing, her mother was living with a boyfriend. This was a culture shock for Vala. She felt that her mother had adopted another culture, dissonant to their Muslim background.

Vala became unruly and belligerent and ran away from her mother's home. She was placed in foster homes. She did not speak the language and didn't feel as though she fit into their Swedish society. In Iraq, she had felt like an outsider because her mother had left her. In Sweden, it was even worse because her mother did not want her. She was incredibly lonely.

Vala continued to go from home to home, until one day she met an older man. He became her world, and she fell head over heels in love with him. Her affections were misplaced, however. He was a drug dealer. At first, Vala would not touch the white powder; but, finally, she succumbed and was hooked. It was all downhill from there. Her life became more and more miserable, and she was in and out of rehab. Vala made multiple suicide attempts. She just wanted to end the pain.

Vala thought that if she had a family, her pain would end. At 26, she found a good man, and they had a son, Sebastian. She loved her son but had no clue about what it took to be a responsible parent. The drugs once again took control of her, and one day she forgot to pick Sebastian up from daycare. She was so high, she just left him there. Vala slit her wrists out of her pain and desperation, but she woke up in a psychiatric hospital. She still did not die. She was so miserable.

Vala had kept in touch with her uncle Samuel, and he was her closest confidant. He had moved to Los Angeles, was very successful, and had invited her to come to join him. He had been attending some group meetings called "Ayahuasca" which was said to help with depression. Vala thought that she would give it a try. What did she have to lose?

It was 2016, and Vala had just been released from another rehab. She went to the first Ayahuasca meeting. Everyone sat in a circle with a shaman. At the beginning, each person was asked what they wanted to experience and what they wanted out of life. Vala said, "I want to know the truth." She remembered writing that she would like to be who she would have become without all of the drug abuse. When the ceremony began, they performed several rituals, including sitting around a fire and drinking an ayahuasca drink. Everyone around her spoke about their wonderful experiences, but it was total misery for Vala.

She attended about eight ceremonies. There was a lot of vomiting (referred to as "purging" by the shaman), lots of confusion, just mayhem. Something was terribly wrong, but she could not figure out exactly what it was. This definitely was not working for her. What was she going to do now? This was her last hope. Or so she thought.

Vala returned to Sweden, then back again to Los Angeles to try Ayahuasca one more time. She remembers that she was screaming. She knew that their lives were in danger. Vala told her uncle Samuel, "Do not take any more drinks. This is dangerous. They are trying to kill us!" But she really did not know who "they" were.

It was at one of these ceremonies, while she was in the midst of darkness and suffering, that she was just screaming. Suddenly, out of nowhere, she felt her hand being lifted, and it touched the area around her heart. For the first time ever, Vala felt the greatest feeling of love that surpassed all human understanding. Someone did care for her. She knew that it was God, the Creator. She sensed that she was in the presence of God. He said to her, "I am with you. Do not be afraid." Then He left. After that encounter, she kept thinking, "Who lifted my hand? Was it a dream?"

Vala decided to go back to Sweden and seek Allah. After all, she had grown up as a Muslim, so she thought that he could help her. She went to the mosque, read the Qur'an, and cried out to Allah for help. Nothing happened. Vala got frustrated, and one day she cried out, "Who are you? Help me! Who are you?" Then she went to sleep, and that night she had a dream. In it, evil spirits were chasing her, and she was running and running. She came to a door, and there was Jesus standing in white clothes with open arms. His countenance had such peace. He took her in His arms and said, "I have already defeated evil. I am the way, the truth, and the life." When He said that, Vala jumped up and hugged Him. She felt an indescribable peace and warmth. Then she woke up. Vala knew that she had seen Jesus.

That dream led her to go to a church where she could find others who worshipped Him. She went to a church and was ecstatic. She had found others who loved Jesus. After a few months of attending her first church, Vala was invited by a friend to visit another church, and she went there. She wanted to go anywhere where she could find Jesus. She began to dedicate her life to His service. Vala had finally found joy and peace.

After about six months, she discovered the Ten Commandments in her Bible. The fourth commandment just seemed to jump out at her:

*"Remember the Sabbath day to keep it holy. Six days shall you labor and do all your work, but the seventh day is the Sabbath of the LORD your God. In it you shall do no work: you, nor your son, nor your daughter, nor your male servant, nor your female servant, nor your cattle, nor your stranger who is within your gates. For in six days the LORD made the heavens and the earth, the sea, and all that is in them, and rested the seventh day. Therefore the LORD blessed the Sabbath day and hallowed it."* (Exodus 20:8–11)

Vala "Googled" information about the seventh-day Sabbath. She could not understand why most of the Christian world went to church on Sunday when Saturday was the seventh day of the week. She adopted the principles and doctrines outlined in the Bible regarding the true Sabbath. Vala left the Sunday church and found a Sabbath-keeping congregation. Then, she began to witness about Jesus to her father and her son, Sebastian. Her father decided to visit her church, and in 2018 was baptized. He, too, is now a Seventh-day Adventist Christian. Sebastian is reading his Bible, and he and Vala are enjoying the best relationship they have ever had. God has restored them. Vala lives for Jesus, and He has set her free.

Finally free. Free from the evil spirits that had plagued her. Free from the depression that had overwhelmed her. She has been redeemed from a life of sin, depression, and loneliness. Yeshua had paid the price for her. He was her Deliverer. Her Redeemer. Her Go'el. Hallelujah!

What about you? Are you feeling trapped, depressed, overwhelmed? Let your Go'el, Jesus Christ, deliver you. Spend more time in His Word, learning about His ways and experiencing more of His love for you. He can walk you through every trial and give you peace in the midst of all your life's storms. Invite Him into your life on a more intimate level and watch how He will deliver you from the things that weigh you down. HE is your Go'el.

## Prayer:

*"Thank You, my **Go'el,** for paying the price for my sins with Your own blood. Thank You for the victory that I can have because You have redeemed me. Please help me to acknowledge the areas of my life that need to be turned over to You, and give me the wisdom to recognize that You and You alone are my Go'el."*

"Not unto us, O Lord, not unto us,
But to Your name give glory,
Because of Your mercy,
Because of Your truth."

—Psalm 115:1

# – Chapter 3 –
# El Shaddai:
# God Almighty
## (ehl shad-dai)
## Alternate Spelling: Shadday

*"But his bow stayed steady, and his arms remained limber because of the help of the Mighty One of Jacob, because of the name of the Shepherd, the Rock of Israel…because of the Shadday who gives you blessings from the heavens above, blessings from the deep springs below the ground, blessings from breasts and womb." (Genesis 49:24–25 NOG)*

In the Holy Scriptures, God revealed Himself to Abram as El Shaddai. He said:

*"I am El Shadday. Live in my presence with integrity. I will give you my promise, and I will give you very many descendants." (Genesis 17:1–2 NOG)*

What about the situation surrounding Abram would warrant God's revelation as El Shaddai, God Almighty? Perhaps it was the fact that Abram was 99 years old when God gave him the promise of being the father of many nations. It was in this conversation that God changed Abram's name to "Abraham," and Sarai's to "Sarah." It was also during this exchange that El Shaddai re-established His covenant and gave circumcision as a sign of that covenant.

This was not the first time that God had interacted with Abram. In Genesis 12:2 (NOG), we find that YHWH tells Abram that He is going to make him a great nation. In His first promise to Abram, YHWH said, *"I will make you a great nation, I will bless you, I will make your name great, and you will be a blessing."*

Abram was 75 years old when he left the land of his birth (Ur of the Chaldeans) to go to Canaan. By the time Abram was 85, he and his wife, Sarai, had taken the matter of having a child into their own hands, and Sarai encouraged Abram to take her servant, Hagar, and have a child with her.

Isn't it ironic that sometimes we get tired of waiting on God? When it seems as though He's not doing anything, because He is not operating on our schedule, we put ourselves into the driver's seat and do what seems right to us. But the Bible says, *"There is a way that seems right to a person, but eventually it ends in death" (Proverbs 14:12 NOG).*

Abram brought himself a lot of grief and conflict by not waiting on the Lord to fulfill His promise. We do the very same thing. We could save ourselves so much hardship if we would just have patience and wait on the Lord, our Elohim, our El Shaddai.

One of the interesting definitions of El Shaddai has to do with sustenance and bountifulness. El is often translated as "God," and primarily means, "might" or "power." Elohim is derived from El, which is translated over two hundred times as "God." [15] Shaddai, in Hebrew, is translated as "almighty." [16] In our Bibles, its root comes from the Hebrew word shad, which means, "breast." [17] It implies power; not of violence, but instead of all-bountifulness. It also suggests, "The Pourer, or Shedder forth of temporal and spiritual blessings." [18]

Andrew Jukes describes Shaddai most beautifully. He says, "His Almightiness is of the breast, that is, of bountiful, self-sacrificing love, giving and pouring itself out for others. Therefore He can quiet the restless as the breast quiets the child: therefore, He can attract, as the breast attracts when we are in peril of falling from Him. This is the Almighty." [19] This is our El Shaddai.

When we call upon El Shaddai, we invoke the One for Whom nothing is impossible. He is the One who pours out blessing upon blessing upon His creatures. But more than just temporal blessings, almightiness is "the power to carry out the will of a Divine nature." [20] According to Jukes, in order to be almighty, God must be able to implement and carry out His own will and purpose to the uttermost. [21] What is His will? To save His creatures and to restore and conform them to His image.

In El Shaddai, the Almighty, we have the "Pourer-forth," Who pours His Spirit into us and shed His lifeblood for us. I love the way Jukes expresses this. He says, "This is 'El Shaddai,' the 'Pourer-forth,' who pours Himself out for His creatures; who gives them His lifeblood; [22] who sheds forth His spirit, [23] and says, 'Come unto me and drink:' [24] 'Open thy mouth wide and I will fill it:' [25] and who, thus, by the sacrifice of Himself, gives Himself and His very nature to those who will receive Him, that thus His perfect will may be accomplished in them." [26]

Nathan Stone, in his book, *Names of God*, states it almost poetically. He said:

> Thus in this name, God is seen to be the power or shedder forth of blessings, the all-sufficient and the all-bountiful One. Of course, the idea of One who is all-powerful and all-mighty is implied in this, for only an all-powerful One could be all-sufficient and all-bountiful. He is almighty because He can carry out His purposes and plans to their fullest and most glorious and triumphant completion. He is able to triumph over every obstacle and over all opposition; that is, He is sufficient for all these things. And He can do exceedingly and abundantly above all that we can ask or think. From all of this, it is felt that the name El Shaddai or God Almighty is much better understood as that El, who is all-sufficient and all-bountiful, the source of all blessing and fullness and fruitfulness.

Ask Dwight. He knows this all too well.

## Dwight's Story

After he rededicated his life to the Lord, God called Dwight into the publishing ministry. He sold the businesses that he was operating with some other family members and started Remnant Publications. Dwight and Deb, his wife, used part of the sale money to launch Remnant and set aside the remainder to live on.

For the first eleven years, he never took a salary from Remnant because the ministry couldn't afford it. They were solely dependent upon God. About that time, Deb and Dwight moved to the wilderness of Montana where there were minimal distractions or amenities to pull them away from God. They had no debt, so they figured that they could live on $13,000 a year.

They had enough money to last for a while, but not indefinitely. Dwight told Deb, who managed the finances, not to worry. "I'll dig ditches by hand to earn money if I have to," he said.

One day, about four years after the move, Deb came to Dwight and said, "You had better buy that shovel." "Why?" He asked, thinking she was joking.

"Because that's about how much money we have left—enough to buy a shovel," she replied. "And you need to start digging some ditches."

"I have a better idea," he told her. "I'm going to see if those dead trees on our property are worth anything."

When they had first moved to their 35-acre property, they had been told that the trees were no good for anything but firewood. But one of the employees at Remnant had recently called in a logger on their own land and had done quite well.

"Maybe you should check into those dead trees," John, the employee, told Dwight. "They are worth more now than they were a few years ago because the market is so good." After praying about their financial situation, Dwight decided to call the same logger to see if they could get some money from the fallen timber on their property.

The logger went out to see Dwight and Deb. His name was Enos, and he was a dedicated Christian.

"I think I can get five semi-truck loads of wood from your dead trees," Enos told them. "I'll be happy to give you $3,750 upfront." That meant $750 per load.

"Well, what if you get more wood than that?" Dwight wanted to know. "How much do you think is here?" Enos asked. "I was hoping for about eight loads," Dwight replied.

Enos shook his head. Having been in this business for years, he had a pretty good idea of how many loads to expect.

"I would be surprised if you get that much," he told them. "For one thing, part of your property is swampy ground and another part is a lake. You will do well if you have even 15 acres of woodland here. And remember, we are only taking the dead trees."

"Yes," Dwight replied. "But what will happen if you get more than you projected?" "I will give you $750 per load," Enos promised. He estimated that it would take his loggers about one week to remove the dead wood from the property.

The loggers came as promised and worked on Dwight and Deb's property for a week. In the meantime, Dwight and Deb were busy praying that they would find lots of dead trees. At the end of the week, Dwight went out to check on their progress.

"We are just about done," they told him. "Just a little bit more to do, so we will be back on Monday morning to finish the job," they said.

Dwight and Deb kept praying. On Monday afternoon, when Dwight went out to check on their progress, the loggers informed him that they had found another stand of dead trees.

"Seems like we missed one," they told him. "We will be back to take that stand on Tuesday, and after that, we will be done." Dwight and Deb kept praying. On Wednesday afternoon when Dwight went to check, they told him the same story.

"Dwight, we just can't understand this," Enos added. "How many places can a dead tree hide? We just finish cutting over here, and then we find more dead trees over there, and on it goes."

Dwight went back to his house rejoicing that afternoon because he knew God was at work. There was no way they could find that many dead trees on their property, and yet they just kept finding them. It reminded Deb and Dwight of the widow and her jar of oil (2 Kings 4:1–7) and the widow whose barrel of meal was continually replenished during a terrible famine (1 Kings 17:8–16).

Enos and his men cut timber on Dwight and Deb's fifteen wooded acres for a full three weeks. Every day they came expecting to finish the job, and every day they found more fallen timber. They finally did quit, but not because they had run out of dead trees. Their other customers were getting upset because Enos was two weeks behind schedule!

During those three weeks, Dwight stood at the window and watched those loads going out with mounting excitement. By the time the loggers were done on their property, they did not have $3,750 for five loads as initially projected, but $13,500 worth of dead trees—that is 18 loads!

That was a real miracle—to get an entire year's income off dead trees and have their woods cleaned up at the same time. They have never forgotten how God provided for them. It was a real turning point in their lives because they realized that if God can make dead trees appear out of nowhere, He can do anything.

Nathan Stone beautifully states:

So we see that the name *Almighty God* speaks to us of the inexhaustible stores of His bounty, of the riches and fullness of His grace in self-sacrificing love pouring itself out for others. It tells us that from God comes every good and perfect gift that

He never wearies of pouring His mercies and blessings upon His people. But we must not forget that His strength is made perfect in our weakness; His sufficiency is most manifest in our insufficiency; His fullness in our emptiness, that being filled, from us may flow rivers of living water to a thirsty and needy humanity. [27]

El Shaddai, The Almighty, the Pourer-Forth, The All-Sufficient One, the One Who provides all our needs, was ever willing to pour forth His blessings upon Dwight and Deb. He can do the same for you.

## Prayer:

"*El Shaddai, Almighty God, You are my Source. It is because of Your blessings that I am prosperous. NOTHING is impossible for You. Your bounty overflows into my life, and I am so grateful for Your provision. Please fill in my areas of lack and help me to always appreciate Your generosity by sharing Your gifts with those in need. Lead me to someone that I can help today.*"

# – Chapter 4 –
# El Tsur:
# God, the Rock
## (ehl-tsur)

*"He is the Rock [El Tsur], His work is perfect; for all His ways are justice. A God of truth and without injustice; righteous and upright is He." (Deuteronomy 32:4)*

Moses made a big mistake at Kadesh. In fact, it was perhaps one of the greatest lapses of judgment in his prophetic leadership. We find the account of this error in Numbers 20. The children of Israel journeyed into the Wilderness of Zin and stayed in Kadesh. It was there that Moses' and Aaron's sister, Miriam, died and was buried.

There was no water there, and the people turned on Moses and Aaron complaining in anger about the living conditions. They asked the brothers why they had brought them and their animals into the wilderness to die. Moses and Aaron sought the Lord for answers, and He told them:

*"Take the rod; you and your brother Aaron gather the congregation together. **Speak to the rock before their eyes, and it will yield its water** (emphasis added); thus you shall bring water for them out of the rock and give drink to the congregation and their animals." (Numbers 20:8)*

The Bible goes on to say that Moses took the rod as God had commanded him to do. But then, Moses gathered the people together and said,

*"Hear now, you rebels! **Must we bring water for you out of this rock** (emphasis added)?" Then Moses lifted his hand and **struck the rock twice with his rod** (emphasis added); and water came out abundantly, and the congregation and their animals drank." (v. 10–11)*

*"Then the LORD spoke to Moses and Aaron, 'Because you did not believe Me, to hallow Me in the eyes of the children of Israel, therefore you shall not bring this assembly into the land which I have given them.'" (v. 12)*

Consider the question that Moses asked the people: "Must *we* bring water for you out of this rock?" Wait a minute. Who was providing the water, Moses and Aaron, or God? Did Moses overstep his bounds here by attributing this miracle to himself and his brother instead of to the Almighty? This is a lesson for us. It is not by **our** might, nor by **our** power, but by the power of the living God that feats for Him are accomplished. When we try to reach our goals through our own works, we miss the mark every time.

Secondly, Moses *struck* the rock, instead of just talking to it, as he had been instructed by God to do. Had Moses obeyed God, there would have been a great lesson here that the Lord was imparting to the people. Our Rock (El Tsur) will provide all our needs. We only need to call upon Him:

*"He shall call upon Me, and I will answer him; I will be with him in trouble; I will deliver him and honor him." (Psalm 91:15)*

Did Moses learn his lesson after the incident in Kadesh? I believe he did. Five times in the "Song of Moses" (Deuteronomy 32:4, 15, 18, 30, 31) the word "Tsur" (Rock) is used as a title of God. [28] Isn't it ironic that Moses would allude to God as "The Rock?" It was from "The Rock" that Moses learned the price that is paid for disobedience. He was not allowed to lead the people into the Promised Land. It is to "The Rock" that he ascribes greatness and honor:

*"For I proclaim the name of the LORD; ascribe greatness to our God. He is the Rock. His work is perfect; for all His ways are justice, a God of truth and without injustice; righteous and upright is He." (Deuteronomy 32:3–4)*

Like a rock, our God is steady, dependable, solid, and strong. There is no other god like our God. Moses knew that, and we must acknowledge that with El Tsur, The Rock, we are anchored and firmly positioned. Without Him, we can do nothing.

An even more personal depiction of El Tsur is found in the story of Hannah, mother of the prophet, Samuel. This story is found in 1 Samuel, chapters 1 and 2.

Hannah was depressed. She could not eat, and she found herself crying a lot. Why couldn't she have a child of her own? Her husband, Elkanah, had another wife, Peninnah who bore him sons. Peninnah taunted Hannah and made her life miserable. Every year, Elkanah took his family to Shiloh to worship and sacrifice to the Lord. Whenever the time came to make an offering, Elkanah would give portions to Peninnah and all her children. The Bible says that Elkanah loved Hannah, and although she was barren, he tried to make it up to her by giving her double portions of offerings.

Year after year, Peninnah would provoke Hannah to the point of despair. One day, while feeling deep anguish, Hannah, in her pain wept and cried out to the Lord. Then she made a vow to Him and said:

*"Oh LORD of hosts, if You will indeed look on the affliction of Your maidservant and remember me, and not forget Your maidservant, but will give Your maidservant a male child, then I will give him to the LORD all the days of his life, and no razor shall come upon his head." (1 Samuel 1:11)*

Hannah was praying so intensely that Eli, the High Priest, saw her lips moving but heard no sound. He thought she was inebriated and chastised her for being drunk. She assured him that she wasn't and shared her sorrow with Eli. He told her to go in peace and pronounced a blessing upon her: *"The God of Israel grant your petition which you have asked of Him"* (1 Samuel 1:17).

When Hannah left Eli, she felt better. She had a sense of peace. After returning home, the Bible says that *"Elkanah knew Hannah his wife, and the LORD [YHWH] remembered her"* (1 Samuel 1:19). Hannah conceived a son, and named him Samuel, because she had asked the Lord for him. What joy she felt. Hannah had known that the only place to turn was to El Tsur, her Rock: her only hope amid her misery. She looked to Him, and He was steady, dependable, and strong. She said:

*"No one is holy like the LORD [YHWH] for there is none besides You, nor is there any rock [Tsur]) like our God [Elohim]." (1 Samuel 2:2)*

A large rock is powerful to behold. It is strong, stable, dependable, and anchored. Our Tsur is mighty, dependable, stable, and anchored. We can hold onto Him for protection from whatever assails us. He is our Rock. When life gets you down, and you think that there is nowhere else to turn, turn to El Tsur, The Lord, your Rock. [29]

## Magna's Story

This life is so unpredictable. Magna received some disturbing news. Her brother was missing. He was 32 years old and a young physician who was at the top of his game. With no prior warning, he just disappeared. For three long years, no one had any idea about what had happened to him. Then, one week before her wedding, he was found dead behind a baseball field. What a bittersweet day it was when she got married. She said that it was only by God's grace that she was able to move forward with her wedding plans.

Some years later, while walking with a friend, she noticed tingling in the fingers on her right hand. Over the next several days, the tingling began to travel up her arm and down her side. What was happening to her? She went to a physician and was diagnosed with multiple sclerosis. What a shock. Was she going to be disabled? How would she navigate through this? Again, she knew that she needed to depend upon the Lord to get her through.

Two years after Magna's diagnosis, it was discovered that her mother, with whom she had a very close relationship, was diagnosed with colon cancer. Her mother passed away six months later.

As if this was not difficult enough, a year and a half after her mother's passing, Magna's husband began to experience some unexplained sensations in his head, and soon afterward, his legs. This progressed to the point where he had difficulty sitting and had leg spasms. Just two days before his scheduled medical evaluation, he had a major seizure and was rushed to the hospital. It was discovered that he had an uncommon congenital disorder known as arteriovenous malformation. He was put into a medically induced coma to protect his brain from further seizures, and he never came out of the coma. His funeral was a week later.

So much loss, back to back. How did Magna make it through? She received strength from El Tsur, her Rock. He nurtured her and held her up through the darkest of times. In the midst of her struggles, El Tsur was there, pouring His mercy on her and giving her His strength to counter her weakness. El Tsur led her to and sustained her with some natural treatments that helped her regain her health. She has had no symptoms of multiple sclerosis for the past 12 years. Magna also gained another wonderful, godly husband who has brought happiness to her life again. El Tsur brought her through her pain and restored her joy. Only El Tsur, our Elohim, can do that.

## Prayer:

*"**El Tsur,** You are my Rock, the only one that I can truly depend on in times of despair. Please give me the strength to hang on during my hardest times and help me to remember that You are my steady, strong, and dependable Rock. I can do all things through Your power."*

---

"Oh Lᴏʀᴅ [YHWH], our Lord [Adonai],
how excellent is Your name in
all the earth, Who have set Your
glory above the heavens!"

–Psalm 8:1

---

# Chapter 5

# YESHUA (JESUS):
# YHWH Is Salvation
## (Yeh-shoo-ah)

*"She will give birth to a son, and you will name*
*him Yeshua [He Saves], because He will save His*
*people from their sins." (Matthew 1:21 NOG)*

What in the world was going on? Joseph had to think that his world was crumbling around him. He was engaged to Mary, and now she was pregnant?! He had never touched her. Surely, she would not betray him like that. Well, he would break the engagement privately and just send her away. He did not want to shame her publicly. How could this have happened? Just while he was thinking about all of this, an angel appeared to him in a dream and said:

*"Joseph, descendant of David, don't be afraid to take Mary as*
*your wife. She is pregnant by the Holy Spirit. She will give birth to*
*a son, and you will name Him Yeshua [He Saves], because He will*
*save His people from their sins." (Matthew 1:20–21 NOG)*

Pregnant by the Holy Spirit? When Joseph woke up, he obeyed the angel and took Mary to be his wife. The Bible says that he did not have marital relations with her until after she gave birth to a son. He named him Yeshua, as per the instructions of the angel.

Yeshua is a shortened form of the name Yahoshua, which we first find in the Old Testament book of Yehoshua, or what we now call "Joshua." Yehoshua is the literal Hebrew word for "Salvation." [30] Yehoshua consists of two parts: [31]

1) "Yeho—" is a shortened form of the Tetragrammaton (YHWH) when it is the first part of a name. The English form is LORD.

2) "—shua" is an abbreviated form of the verb yasha, which means "to save, rescue, or deliver." Thus, the name Yehoshua means "the LORD saves or delivers."

The ancient name for Jesus was Yeshua. That was the name that He was probably called as a child growing up in His home. Although it was rather conventional at that time, when applied to the Lord it was a name that had a unique and special significance.

Yeshua is the Savior of the world. Many people want to say that there are many roads to God, but the Bible teaches that there is only one way and that is through our Yeshua, the Lord Jesus Christ.

*"There is salvation [Heb. yeshuah] in no one else; for there is no other Name under heaven that has been given among men, by which we must be saved." (Acts 4:12)* [32]

Interestingly, many today do not want to acknowledge sin. They think that to do so is to insult people or demean them in some way. There are even some evangelical preachers who will not preach about the cross, repentance, or the blood of Jesus. That suits Satan just fine. If we cannot call sin by its proper name, then we cannot realize our need for a Savior.

Someone had to pay the price for humanity's sin. Someone had to remove the wall of separation that sin creates between us and our Creator, our Elohim.

How wonderful to have a God who would assume our form, live a sinless and holy life, allow Himself to be crucified in order to pay the price for the sins of humankind, and then promise to return to take us home with Him. If you want to get a good sense of who Yeshua was and is, read the gospels in the New Testament: Matthew, Mark, Luke, and John. They outline His birth, life, death, and resurrection. They explain His purpose and mission. He loves everyone, no matter how distant they may feel from Him. Yeshua said that He came to seek and to save that which was lost. Is that you?

One day, Yeshua is going to return to take us home with Him. On that day, even those who rejected Him will have to acknowledge who He really is:

*"God highly exalted him, and bestowed on him **the Name** which is above every name, that at the name of **Yeshua** ['the LORD saves*

*or delivers'] every knee should bow, of those who are in heaven, and on earth, and under the earth, and that every tongue should confess that **Yeshua** Messiah is Lord, to the glory of God the Father." (Philippians 2:9–11)* [33]

When we read in the Bible about Yeshua (Jesus), we realize the power that He has, not only to save but to transform. Not only to transform but to deliver us from the evil forces that seek to destroy us. Samuel had to find this out for himself.

## Samuel's Story

Samuel knew that he was gay at a very young age. Born in Iraq Kurdistan, into a Muslim family, he knew that his same-sex attraction was socially tabooed. At 15, Samuel moved to Sweden as a refugee. He thought that he would, at last, be happy and able to live his life freely as a gay man. Instead, he became more and more depressed.

Eleven years later, Samuel packed his bags and moved to Los Angeles where he lived for about 17 years. It was in Los Angeles that he became recognized as the 24th most successful realtor in the nation. It was there, in Los Angeles, that Samuel lived the "high life" with private jets, multiple lovers, and lots of money. But he could not have been more unhappy.

He began to look for happiness and peace in the New Age movement. He did yoga, practiced Transcendental Meditation, tried hypnosis, and even became a level 3 Reiki Master. He was still miserable.

One night, he was at a party with his boyfriend at the time, when he met a handsome guy who said that he had left homosexuality and had given his life to Jesus Christ. Samuel thought to himself, "Poor guy, someone has brainwashed him." Samuel, by his own admission, was a proud gay man who would get angry if anyone implied that homosexuality was something to be saved from.

Six months later, his niece, Vala, who had been struggling with drug addiction since she was 13, also said that she had met Jesus Christ. She was one of Samuel's closest friends, and he witnessed how she was set free from all depression and drug use. It was a real miracle.

This really got Samuel thinking that maybe he too should get to know Jesus. If Jesus could help the guy at the party and set his niece free from drugs and depression, could He do the same thing for him?

Samuel decided to surrender his life to Jesus Christ, and he says it is the best decision that he ever made. He said that he has never had more peace and joy in his life than he does now. Samuel said:

"The peace and joy that I have since I have been saved surpasses all human understanding. I do not miss anything from my old life. Jesus Christ has given me victory over homosexuality. When I tell people that I have repented from homosexuality and follow Christ, many feel sorry for me. They think that I am denying my identity or that I turned my back on the gay community. But the truth is that God has saved me from a life of pain and selfishness and self-destruction. I wish more people would give Jesus a chance."

One of my favorite Bible verses is, "I count all things but loss for the excellency of the knowledge of Christ Jesus my Lord: For whom I have suffered the loss of all things, and do count them but dung, that I may win Christ." (Philippians 3:8 KJV)

Only Yeshua, Jesus, has the power to change a life. He removes despair and replaces it with joy and peace. Samuel found out for himself. What about you? Do you want to find out for yourself just what Yeshua has to offer? Romans 10:9–10 says:

*"If you confess with your mouth the Lord Jesus and believe in your heart that God has raised Him from the dead, you will be saved. For with the heart one believes unto righteousness, and with the mouth confession is made unto salvation."*

You may have been given this book as a gift, or you may have picked it up somewhere. Just know that it is no coincidence that you are reading it. Whether you are a seasoned Christian, or a curious agnostic, renewing or accepting Yeshua as your Savior is life changing.

Samuel saw the transforming power of the Lord, as demonstrated in his formerly gay acquaintance, and in his previously drug-addicted and depressed niece, Vala (whose testimony is also in this book). Samuel made a decision to give Yeshua a try, and it is a decision that he has not regretted. Won't you decide for Yeshua today? What do you have to lose? You will not regret it, and I promise your life will never be the same again.

## Prayer:

*"Dear **Yeshua,** I have parts of my life that need to be changed. I need to recognize those areas and then turn them over to You so that You can transform me. If there is something that I want to hold on to, please help me to want to let it go. I cannot do that on my own. Please save me from the sins that surround me and give me Your peace."*

"His name shall endure forever;
His name shall continue as long as the sun.
And men shall be blessed in Him;
All nations shall call Him blessed."

—Psalm 72:17

# – Chapter 6 –
# El Mekaddesh:
# The God Who Sanctifies
## (Ehl-meh-kad-desh)

*"Surely My Sabbaths you shall keep, for it is a sign between Me and you throughout your generations, that you may know that I am the LORD [YHWH] who sanctifies you." (Exodus 31:13)*

W hat does it mean to be sanctified? According to *Baker's Evangelical Dictionary of Biblical Theology*:

> The generic meaning of sanctification is 'the state of proper functioning.' To sanctify someone or something is to set that person or thing apart for the use intended by its designer. A pen is 'sanctified' when used to write. Eyeglasses are 'sanctified' when used to improve sight. In the theological sense, people are sanctified when they are used for the purpose God intends. A human being is sanctified, therefore, when he or she lives according to God's design and purpose. [34]

Another definition of sanctified is "to be set apart for holy use." [35]

It is interesting to note that in Exodus 31:13, The LORD (YHWH) connects the keeping of the Sabbath to the identification of Him Who sanctifies. It involves living according to His divine purpose for your life. In the book, *Education*, author Ellen White states:

> The Sabbath is a sign of creative and redeeming power; it points to God as the source of life and knowledge; it recalls man's primeval glory, and thus witnesses to God's purpose to re-create us in His own image. [36]

The Sabbath is a time of spiritual renewal and refreshing. This is when we put aside our mundane daily activities and more earnestly seek God's ways and His will. The Sabbath is the day on which we have corporate and individual worship, plugging into the Ultimate Source of our power, our Elohim. What we often fail to realize is that the Sabbath is our "re-charge day." It is the time in which we renew our relationship with God.

While every day is essential for spiritual focus, the seventh-day Sabbath (Saturday) is the day on which Elohim has placed a special blessing. Genesis 2:3 (NOG) says, *"Then Elohim blessed the seventh day and set it apart as holy because on that day He stopped all His work of creation."*

What, then, is the importance of the Sabbath? It establishes the identity of our Creator and the One Who re-creates us into the image of our God, our Elohim. Therefore, as we remember the Sabbath and keep it holy, we are acknowledging the one True God and Creator of the universe. He, El Mekaddesh, is the One Who sets us apart for His sacred use. He is the God Who sanctifies us.

In order to experience sanctification, we must consecrate ourselves to God. Leviticus 20:7–8 says:

> *"Consecrate yourselves therefore, and be holy, for I am the LORD [YHWH] your God. And you shall keep My statutes, and perform them: I am the LORD [YHWH] Who sanctifies you."*

How can we consecrate ourselves to God? We can give Him our will. The Lord wants our minds and bodies to be consecrated to Him. It is not enough to sit back and wait for the Holy Spirit to do it. We play a part in all of this as well. We must yield our will to Him to be shaped, molded, and conformed into the likeness of Yeshua (Jesus), the Savior. He will never force obedience upon us, but He will guide us in the right direction. We can spend time with Him in Bible study and prayer so that He can speak to us, and His Holy Spirit will chip away at "self" so that we begin to act like and represent Yeshua in the world around us.

Paul, in Romans 12:1–2, tells us how to consecrate ourselves fully to God. He says:

> *"I beseech you therefore, brethren, by the mercies of God, that you present your bodies a living sacrifice, holy acceptable to God, which is your reasonable service. And do not be conformed to this world, but be transformed by the renewing of your mind, that you may prove what is that good and acceptable and perfect will of God."*

The work of sanctification is the work of a lifetime. Ellen White said, "Sanctification is not the work of a moment, an hour, a day, but of a lifetime. It is not gained by a happy flight of feeling, but is the result of constantly dying to sin, and constantly living for Christ."[37] It is not by our righteousness or our power that we can have victory over sin. The Bible says,"*Not by might nor by power, but by My Spirit, says the* LORD *of hosts" (Zechariah 4:6).*

As we daily seek the Lord and His righteousness, He will do something marvelous in us.

> *"I will give you a new heart and put a new spirit in you; I will remove from you your heart of stone and give you a heart of flesh. And I will put my Spirit in you and move you to follow my decrees and be careful to keep my laws." (Ezekiel 36:26–27 NIV)*

This is the best heart surgery that there ever could be.

We can rest assured that the work of sanctification will be accomplished in us as we surrender our will to God.

> *"Being confident of this very thing, that He who has begun a good work in you will complete it until the day of Jesus Christ." (Philippians 1:6)*

Check out how Loto's life has been transformed through the power of the Holy Spirit.

## Loto's Story

Lotolua (also known as "Loto") was an assassin for a drug cartel. He had no conscience and looked at people as though they were just objects, not human beings. He'd had a rocky road growing up. The ninth of eleven children, Loto was his dad's favorite child. In fact, he was never spanked or disciplined at all by his father. His father was a god to him. Loto wanted to please him and make him proud.

Tragedy struck when his father was killed by a drunk driver when Loto was only nine years old. He became angry and began acting out. He hated the world.

During his first eleven years in Samoa, Loto's family held a high position of honor. The young men in Samoan Island families would often fight each other to determine dominance and power. Loto began to challenge other young (and older) boys. He never lost a fight. He was angry and violent, and the fighting magnified it even more. Violence became second nature to him.

When he was almost twelve years old, his mother took him to the United States to live. It was here that Loto joined a gang. He was able to see what gang life with its violence was all about.

After a while, Loto decided that he had had enough of gang life, so he joined the United States military. It was after the military that he started selling drugs. Loto had wanted to be a policeman, but he began to hang out with the wrong crowd, and he saw how he could make a lot of money in the drug world. He began to sell them himself.

It was during that time that he had a serious car accident. While he was healing, a friend invited him to come to Washington to get better. Loto moved to Washington state, and that is where his drug dealing and violence escalated. He discovered that he had to really be tough to control his territory. Different "families" of gangs (Bloods, Crips, etc.) controlled the cartel. They ran distribution lines from Texas to Oklahoma, to Colorado, to California, to Oregon and Washington. Loto moved product and removed anyone who got in his or his drug cartel's way.

Loto became known as "Ice" because he was cold in his dealings with others. Ice was an eliminator who felt as though he was the best at what he did. After he targeted his mark, or victim, cleaners would come in and get rid of all evidence. He had a reputation for being very mean, cold, and thorough and he relished that.

While Loto was building his assassin reputation, his mother, a mighty prayer warrior, was praying and fasting for him. She pleaded with God to "make Loto miserable in his sins. Don't let him enjoy his sin."

Whenever the upper echelon tiers of the cartel finished moving product (drugs), they would take a vacation somewhere and celebrate. On this particular day, after one such celebration, Loto discovered he had locked his keys in his car. He had some of his workers attempt to get into the car for him while he waited inside.

Loto was alone and was sniffing cocaine when he distinctly heard a loud voice say, "Come home!" He began to have paranoid thoughts like someone had given him some harmful drugs. Maybe someone was trying to set him up. He then thought that perhaps this was some sort of supernatural phenomenon. Was God talking to him? He looked and saw a dark shadow leaving his body and leaving him. It was as though an evil spirit was coming out of him. Loto began to cry. Before this, he never believed in the spirit world. This encounter was real.

Shortly after that, he received a flyer in the mail about an evangelistic series being held in his area, and he attended the meetings. It was at these meetings that he first really encountered Jesus and gave his heart to Him. These meetings were very special to Loto. It was there that the Holy Spirit convicted him about the Sabbath.

The seventh-day Sabbath (from sunset on Friday until sundown on Saturday) has played an enormous role in Loto's life. He said, "I long for the Sabbath. It makes me feel like I am home. It separates me from the world. There is a special connection that I feel to God during that time. There is something about the Sabbath that makes me feel as though I am entering into the holiness of God. I feel like I catch a glimpse of what Heaven is going to be like."

Loto has been cherishing and keeping the Sabbath ever since he gave his heart to the Lord during the evangelistic series. He feels as though it brings him closer to God. Loto decided to live his life for Him, and Him only, but God was not finished with Loto.

The Holy Spirit impressed him to turn himself in to the law to pay for his crimes. Loto did just that and received a twenty-year sentence for his one charge of first-degree murder. That, in and of itself, was an act of God because he should have been charged with two counts. He served seventeen and a half years (two and a half years were taken off for good behavior).

While in prison, Loto faithfully watched 3ABN and was discipled in the ways of the Lord by watching it. He is now a prominent member of his church, married, and serving God with all his might. He shares his testimony, the beauty of the Sabbath, and the power of God with all who will listen. Loto's life has been transformed by El Mekaddesh, the God who sanctifies us. He purifies us and sets us apart for His service. Glory be to our El Mekaddesh.

## Prayer:

*"Dear El Mekaddesh, I need to be changed by You. I need to know that You can use me, as damaged as I am, in Your service. Please show me the best way to serve You. Re-charge me on Your*

*holy Sabbath. Set me apart for Your service, and give me a new life, starting right here, and right now. I am available to You. Please fix and fit me for Your kingdom."*

# Chapter 7

# El HaNe'eman:
# Faithful God
## (Ehl-hah-ne-e-mahn)

*"Keep in mind that Yahweh [YHWH] your Elohim is
the only Elohim. He is a faithful El [El-HaNe'eman],
who keeps His promise and is merciful to thousands
of generations of those who love Him and obey
His commands." (Deuteronomy 7:9 NOG)*

I t was the end of 40 years of wandering through the wilderness when
the new generation was on the verge of entering the promised land
of Canaan. Moses summoned the people to talk to them. He knew
that he would be unable to accompany them to their final destination
because of his sin. Still, he had to give them some encouragement and
admonishments to support them in the last segment of their journey.

Moses reminded them of how God had led them through the wilderness, providing for and protecting them. In Deuteronomy 2:7, Moses
told the people that Elohim had blessed them in everything they had
done. He said:

*"For the LORD [YHWH] your God has blessed you in all the
work of your hand. He knows your trudging through this great
wilderness. These forty years the LORD [YHWH] your God has
been with you: you have lacked nothing."*

He reminded them that their Elohim had watched over them as
they traveled through this vast desert. For 40 years now, YHWH, their
Elohim, had been with them, and they had not needed a thing. He
admonished them to be loyal to YHWH. In Deuteronomy 7:3, Moses
tells them not to intermarry with those who worship idols because they
would turn God's people's hearts against Him. They were to obey His
commands, laws, and rules. Verses 12 and 13 (NOG) say:

*"If you listen to these rules and faithfully obey them, Yahweh [YHWH] your Elohim will keep His promise to you and be merciful to you, as He swore to your ancestors. He will love you, bless you, and increase the number of your descendants. He will bless you with children. He will bless your land with produce: grain, new wine, and olive oil. He will bless your herds with calves, and your flocks with lambs and kids. This will all happen in the land Yahweh [YHWH] will give you, as He swore to your ancestors."*

It is interesting to me that this passage refers to a promise made by YHWH years before these Israelites were around. He had made this promise to the ancestors of that generation. God honors His commitments to His children, and multiple generations will benefit from it. What an amazing God. What a faithful Father.

*"O Yahweh [YHWH], your word is established in heaven forever. Your faithfulness endures throughout every generation. You set the earth in place, and it continues to stand." (Psalm 119:89–90 NOG)*

In my own life, I know that the relationship that my grandmothers, Rosa Lee Jones and Zelma Hodge, had with the Lord paved the way for me. Their prayers for my children and me "followed them," even after their deaths. God has honored my grandmothers' and my parents' prayers by bringing my children and me back to Him.

Not only is God faithful to our parents and grandparents, He is faithful to us in our everyday dealings with Him. He is constantly working for our good behind the scenes— protecting us, providing for us, and most importantly, sanctifying us by His Holy Spirit. Paul, in a prayer for the Thessalonians, shares this idea beautifully. He said:

*"Now may the God of peace Himself sanctify you completely: and may your whole spirit, soul and body be preserved blameless at the coming of our Lord Jesus Christ. He who calls you is faithful, who also will do it." (1 Thessalonians 5:23–24)*

Our God, our El HaNe'eman, is faithful throughout our generations. Here is just a glimpse into what He has done for me:

## Yvonne's Story

I was raised in a Christian home with Christian parents, but it was the influence of my grandmothers (particularly my maternal grandmother, Rosa Lee Jones, with whom I lived for some time) that had the most profound impact on my walk with Christ. My mother died when I was 19 years old, and after she passed, my grandmothers stepped in to help my little sister, "Binky," [38] and me.

I stayed in the church for a while but drifted out after I got involved with the entertainment industry as a studio singer. My grandmothers were really concerned about Binky and me, and they could see us getting further and further away from the Lord.

I got married and had a son, Marc. He was precious. My first-born! He was handsome and very strong-willed. Early on, instead of us training him, Marc taught his father and me. He knew how to get our attention and how to get his way. He would cry until one of us picked him up (usually it was his dad) and with his dad's impatience heightened, the only way that Marc would stop is if he were picked up. Oh he trained us, alright. His strong-willed nature continued into his teens.

During Marc's early school years, I gave him everything that money could buy: designer clothes, the latest toys, and every kind of lesson that his heart desired (including computer lessons, tennis lessons, karate lessons, and drum lessons). At that time, I had a very successful career in the music business. Money was plentiful, and I gave him the best that money could buy.

Do you get the picture? Marc was a privileged child. But the one thing, the most important thing that I did not teach him was a dependence upon God. He did not have a real relationship with Jesus because I did not have one myself. I was financially independent and spiritually bankrupt.

My dear grandmother, Rosa Lee Jones, took Marc to church every Sabbath (Saturday) while I slept in. Marc enjoyed the church environment and loved being with his "Mama." I was happy that he was being taken to church, and I felt that he was receiving some spiritual guidance from it although I was not going myself.

The fact is that during his childhood years, I was not a strong spiritual influence in Marc's life. By the time he was a teenager, he was more influenced by his peers and father, who was not a Christian. By the time he was 18, Marc was hanging out with some questionable associates: drug dealers, to be exact. By then, I had been divorced from Marc's dad, re-married, and had another son, Jason. Also, I had re-committed my life to Jesus Christ and was grateful to God for His faithfulness in bringing me back to Him.

One day, a friend of mine from church called me and told me that Marc was hanging out with a lawless crowd and selling drugs. I was devastated. I fell on my knees before God and cried out to Him, begging Him to save my son and not to let him die in his sins. Tears were streaming down my face as I pleaded for Marc's salvation.

You see, I know how the enemy works. He wanted to kill my son and remove all hope for his salvation. That day, I went into intercessory prayer mode. I remember crying before God when He clearly spoke to me and repeated Isaiah 49:25 (KJV): *"For I will contend with him that contendeth with thee, and I will save thy children."*

I immediately stopped crying. The Lord Himself had just spoken to me and had reassured me that He was going to save my children. What a blessing. I no longer had to be distressed about Marc (or later, Jason) because there in that instant, El HaNe'eman, the Faithful God, had seen me in my distress and had come to encourage me.

For the next two decades, I watched my son, Marc, go through some challenging times. He had odd jobs but did not have a trade or a skill that would help him to be independent. Not only that, but he went through a very dark period spiritually, in which he embraced Luciferian ideology.

I could not believe how twisted his impressions of God were. Yet, I knew that God had promised me that He was going to save him, and I held on to that. Marc used certain recreational drugs and was really miserable and broke. He felt that God existed, but that any strides that man made were his own efforts and not God's intervention on any level.

One of my friends suggested that we pray every day at noon for Marc, and that is what we did. I set my alarm for noon and began at that specific time of day to pray for Marc.

It took Marc's hitting rock bottom to lead him to Christ. He had been in a Christian rehab center where he learned to have daily worship. He left the drug program and by that time began to look at God differently. He began to feel God's presence and sensed that He was answering his prayers. This strengthened Marc's faith, and little by little he began to seek God.

Marc realized that he had a distorted view of Jesus and made a choice to get to know the real Jesus of the Bible. How rewarding this has been. Marc now claims Jesus as his Savior and has taken studies toward baptism. He has been sharing the gospel with others and looks forward to Jesus' return.

I just cannot believe the faithfulness of God, my El HaNe'eman. He continues to answer the prayers of His resting saints (my parents and grandparents who prayed earnestly for our salvation), and He cares about our children. He is our precious, reliable, trustworthy, El HaNe'eman, the Faithful God.

El HaNe'eman is there for you, as well. He is a Faithful God, Who longs to save us and our loved ones who don't know Him. Take some time today and think of the many ways in which He has demonstrated His faithfulness in your life. Acknowledge His faithfulness in your journey and be on the lookout for continued manifestations of His love and care.

## Prayer:

*"Oh, **El HaNe'eman,** how faithful You have been to me. I know that You will keep Your promises, and even if it does not happen when I would like it to, You are not on my timetable. You do things in Your way and in Your time. You are ever working to save our children and us. Send Your Holy Spirit to work on them. Help them to see their need of You. Please save my children and loved ones who do not know You for themselves. Help them to see that You are El HaNe'eman, the Faithful God."*

"Praise the LORD!
Praise, O servants of the LORD,
Praise the name of the LORD!
Blessed be the name of the LORD
From this time forth and forevermore!
From the rising of the sun to its going down
The LORD's name *is* to be praised."

–Psalm 113:1-3

# Chapter 8

# YHWH Tsidkenu (Written)
# Adonai Tsidkenu:
# The Lord, Our Righteousness (Spoken)
## (A-doe-nai-tsid-keh-noo)

*"In those days Judah will be saved and Jerusalem
will live securely. Jerusalem will be called
Yahweh [YHWH] Tsidqenu." (Jeremiah 33:16 NOG)*

T he name, "YHWH Tsidkenu" is found only two times in the Bible:
Jeremiah 23:6, and Jeremiah 33:16. Jeremiah 23:5–6 says:

> *"'Behold, the days are coming,' says the LORD [YHWH], 'That I
> will raise to David a Branch of righteousness; A King shall reign
> and prosper, and execute judgment and righteousness in the
> earth. In His days Judah will be saved, and Israel will dwell safely;
> Now this is His name by which He will be called: THE LORD
> OUR RIGHTEOUSNESS.'" [YHWH TSIDKENU]*

This is a Messianic prophecy given to Jeremiah the prophet by the
Lord Himself. He has always provided a deliverer to His people in times
of struggle and hardship, culminating with the Ultimate Deliverer,
Jesus Christ (Yeshua). Jeremiah ministered during a time of great apos-
tasy by the people of Judah. He was called to be YHWH's messenger to
them, bringing messages of judgment and hope to a backsliding people.

In Jeremiah 23, YHWH gives a warning to the spiritual leaders
of that time. He tells them through Jeremiah that as shepherds, they
have *"scattered His flock, driven them away, and not attended to them"*
(verse 2). He warns them and tells them that He will attend to them for
what they have done. [39]

YHWH is serious about taking care of His people. Those in spiritual leadership have a responsibility to care for the flock assigned to
them. The situation was so bad, that YHWH had to let them know
that one day He would raise up "... *a King who will reign and prosper,*

*and execute judgment and righteousness in the earth"* (v. 5). [40] This King would be called, "THE LORD OUR RIGHTEOUSNESS" (v. 6). [41]

Have you ever considered how "unrighteous" you are? No matter how much you try, you realize that you just do not seem to measure up spiritually. Well, praise God that you are thinking that way because you now know that you need a Savior. You need One whose righteousness so exceeds yours that there is no measuring it. You need YHWH Tsid-kenu: The Lord Our Righteousness.

You see, we could never repay the sin debt, primarily because we keep on sinning. We have no righteousness of our own. Romans 3:10–12 says:

*"There is none righteous, no, not one; there is none who understands; there is none who seeks after God. They have all turned aside; they have together become unprofitable; there is none who does good, no, not one."*

That is a dismal thought, isn't it? We often think of others as more holy than they really may be. So, next time you are tempted to think that your church member friend is a sinless saint, remember that they are struggling with some issues just like you are, and need Jesus just as much (if not more) than you do.

In Romans 3:21–26, Paul lays out the issue of righteousness by faith for us. He said:

*"But now the righteousness of God apart from the law is revealed, being witnessed by the Law and the Prophets, even the righteousness of God, through faith in Jesus Christ, to all and on all who believe. For there is no difference; for all have sinned and fall short of the glory of God, being justified freely by His grace through the redemption that is in Christ Jesus, whom God set forth as a propitiation by His blood, through faith, to demonstrate His righteousness, because in His forbearance God had passed over the sins that were previously committed, to demonstrate at the present time His righteousness, that He might be just and the justifier of the one who has faith in Jesus."*

In case that is unclear to you, here are verses 22–26 from the *Life Application Bible* [42]:

*"We are made right with God by placing our faith in Jesus Christ. And this is true for everyone who believes, no matter who we are. For everyone has sinned; we all fall short of God's glorious standard. Yet God, in his grace, freely makes us right in his sight. He did this through Christ Jesus when he freed us from the penalty for our sins. For God presented Jesus as the sacrifice for sin. People are made right with God when they believe that Jesus sacrificed his life, shedding his blood. This sacrifice shows that God was being fair when he held back and did not punish those who sinned in times past, for he was looking ahead and including them in what he would do in this present time. God did this to demonstrate his righteousness, for he himself is fair and just, and he makes sinners right in his sight when they believe in Jesus."*

So, how do we obtain this righteousness? We must YIELD in obedience to the Holy Spirit. Romans 6:16–18 says:

*"Do you not know that to whom you present yourselves slaves to obey, you are that one's slaves whom you obey, whether of sin leading to death, or of obedience leading to righteousness? But God be thanked that though you were slaves of sin, yet you obeyed from the heart that form of doctrine to which you were delivered. And having been set free from sin, you became slaves of righteousness."*

Paul here is stating that we are going to be slaves either to sin or to righteousness. Whoever we present ourselves to, is whom we are going to serve: God or Satan. We can praise God that He will deliver us and set us free from the slavery of sin, but we must sincerely follow Christ and obey His teachings (through the power given to us by His Holy Spirit).

Ellen White said: "The moment a sinner accepts Christ by faith, that moment, he is pardoned. The righteousness of Christ is imputed to him, and he is no more to doubt God's forgiving grace." [43] It is our relationship with, and reliance upon Christ that will save us. His righteousness alone is the key to our "right doing" and "right being."

It is because of what Jesus has done for us on the cross of Calvary. He took our sinfulness upon Himself so that His righteousness could be applied to us. What an exchange. This is a freeing concept. It is not by our works that we are pardoned for our sins. We do not have to be "good enough" to come to Yeshua and be saved by Him. We will never be good enough to come to Him, for it is not OUR goodness that is the issue. It is HIS goodness. We do not have to repeat ten "Hail Marys" or do penance. We just must trust in the saving power of Yeshua. He alone is righteous. He alone can save us.

It is through the power of the Holy Spirit that you go from victory to victory. This is the process of sanctification, which is the work of a lifetime. Our Savior, Yeshua (Jesus), lived a perfect life and His righteousness, when we accept Him as our Savior, is attributed to us. Then, as we continue to seek Him, He continues to impart His righteousness to us, helping us to grow in our spiritual journey.

When YHWH looks at us, He then sees the imparted righteousness of His Son in us. What a gift to know that we have the righteousness of Yeshua to depend upon, instead of our own.

Sometimes, we just cannot seem to climb out from under our bondage. We must come to the place where we realize that it is impossible to address it without Divine intervention. We need YHWH Tsidkenu. Mike had to come to that realization for himself:

## Mike's Story

Mike's mom was a quiet girl who had grown up in a dysfunctional home. Mike's dad was abusive and a jazz musician in the military, gone many months at a time. Mike was often alone with his mother and three sisters.

At an age where it is essential to bond with his gender, Mike chose his mother's identity over his father's. Daddy was mean. Mommy was kind. Mike wanted to be like his mother. He played with dolls and dreamed of becoming a girl. He prayed that God would make him a girl. He really thought that would fix the problem.

Puberty brought on same-sex attraction and masturbation. Feeling inadequate as a male, Mike's only thoughts were that he would be accepted as a woman. During his years in high school, he had a homosexual encounter. He remembers being devastated that it felt so right. At the same time, he felt forsaken and condemned by God. Mike cried himself to sleep.

By the age of 17, Mike prayed that God would take his life so that he would not go into the gay identity, but when God did not, he felt more rejection. He thought that he was not even worth protecting. Mike left the church and blew the doors wide open to the gay culture. His first lover introduced him to sexual perversion, and he became an addict. In 20 years, Mike was never faithful in long-term relationships. On an average day he had as many as three illicit encounters.

Some years and many rendezvous later, Mike was dating a handsome millionaire boyfriend, and they both were making lots of money. By then, Mike had a thriving hair salon and was a much sought-after hair stylist. He was totally invested in the gay culture. Mike felt that he was too far gone to ever return to God. "After all," he thought, "He abandoned me."

Mike did not know that all along, his sisters had been praying for him. They always showed him love and acceptance. "I believe those prayers protected me from AIDS. I should be dead," Mike says.

One day, Mike was invited by his sisters to attend an evangelistic series. He decided to go and see what the preacher was talking about. That day changed Mike's life forever. The sermon was a real gospel message that was so powerful it spoke straight to his heart. In his last appeal the preacher said, "Some of you will never have another opportunity to give your heart to Jesus." Mike felt that his life was so vile that he could not go forward, but the next moment he was down front, giving his heart to the Lord.

This was a journey that would take years. "God had to address the wounds from when I was a child," Mike said. "He stayed with me on this journey, graciously covering me with His righteousness. I was a sex addict in a gay relationship, and I felt that I was born this way."

When Mike began reading God's word, he came across passages about how homosexual behavior was an abomination to God. "How could you make me gay and then call me an abomination?" he thought. "If He wanted me out of my relationship, He was going to have to do it Himself. Once I permitted Him to work, within a few weeks, my boyfriend was gone. I was in anguish. What did God have in store for me? Would I never love again?"

God led Mike to information and scriptures to help deal with lust, addictions, memory, and history. He realized it was not his work, but "Christ working in me." It was YHWH Tsidkenu's righteousness, and not Mike's, that was the saving factor.

*"Let this mind be in you which was also in Christ Jesus."*
*(Philippians 2:5)*

Mike's part was to let the mind of Christ come in and to cooperate with it. It was Christ's job to fight the devil, not Mike's. It was His righteousness that would cover Mike. Mike finally began to gain the victory that had once been so elusive.

As Jesus addressed his broken masculinity, the same-sex attractions began to fade and heterosexual desires started to develop. Mike realized that pornography and masturbation were keeping him from an intimate relationship with God and others.

God calls us to holiness; heterosexuality is a gift from Him. *"Be holy for I am holy" (1 Peter 1:16).*

Mike continues to lean on the power and might of YHWH Tsidkenu for victory. Now, Mike shares his story with others as he ministers to those ensnared in sexual sin. He co-founded "Coming Out Ministries," and he has never looked back. Mike knows that he must continue to rely on the righteousness of His Savior because he is powerless on his own.

What about you? Are you relying on Christ's righteousness to give you victory? Are you struggling with a problem that seems insurmountable, and you are close to giving up because you just don't see any hope? Why not begin today to acknowledge His power to change your attitudes and appetites? He is just waiting for you to invite Him into your life.

## Prayer:

*"**Adonai Tsidkenu,** I am struggling with an addictive behavior that I cannot shake. Please give me Your righteousness and victory over this problem. It is too big for me. I know that I stand before you as a sinner, but You have promised me Your righteousness. I claim it today, this very moment. Thank You, Adonai Tsidkenu, for Your righteousness which will empower me to overcome all temptations. I praise and thank You."*

# – Chapter 9 –
# Immanuel: God Is With Us
## (Ee-ma-noo-ehl)
## (Alternate Spelling: Emmanuel)

*"So Adonay Himself will give you this sign: A virgin will become pregnant and give birth to a son, and she will name Him Immanuel [God Is With Us]." (Isaiah 7:14 NOG)*

King Ahaz was a creep. That got your attention, didn't it? Perhaps I am wrong to call him a name, but he really made some dumb decisions. 2 Kings 16:2–4 says:

*"Ahaz was twenty years old when he became king, and he reigned sixteen years in Jerusalem; and he did not do what was right in the sight of the LORD his God, as his father David had done. But he walked in the way of the kings of Israel; indeed he made his son pass through the fire, according to the abominations of the nations whom the LORD had cast out from before the children of Israel. And he sacrificed and burned incense on the high places, on the hills, and under every green tree."*

Ahaz turned his back on God and worshipped false gods. He even burned his children in the fire as the heathens did. The Bible says that Ahaz encouraged moral decline in Judah and had been continually unfaithful to the Lord. [44]

During Ahaz's reign, Rezin, the king of Syria, and Pekah, king of Israel, decided to come together against him. In a panic and instead of going to God, Ahaz reached out to Tiglath-Pileser, the king of Assyria, and asked him to save him from this deadly alliance. Tiglath-Pileser came to him and "distressed him" (2 Chronicles 28:20).

Ahaz took part of the treasures from the Lord's temple, from his own house, and the homes of the country's leaders and gave them to the king, hoping for his aid. Tiglath-Pileser took the treasures but did not assist Ahaz. Ahaz and his people were terrified. What was he going to do?

It was then that YHWH told Isaiah to take his son, Shear-Jashub, and go to meet Ahaz and say to him:

*"Take heed, and be quiet; do not fear or be fainthearted for these two stubs of smoking firebrands, for the fierce anger of Rezin and Syria, and the sons of Remaliah. Because Syria, Ephraim, and the son of Remaliah have plotted evil against you, saying, 'Let us go up against Judah and trouble it, and let us make a gap in its wall for ourselves, and set a king over them, the son of Tabel' —*

*"Thus says the* LORD *God:*

*"It shall not stand, nor shall it come to pass. For the head of Syria is Damascus, and the head of Damascus is Rezin. Within sixty-five years Ephraim will be broken so that it will not be a people. The head of Ephraim is Samaria, and the head of Samaria is Remaliah's son. If you will not believe, surely you shall not be established." (Isaiah 7:4–9)*

Right after this, YHWH did a beautiful thing. He invited Ahaz to ask a sign for himself. He said, *"Ask Yahweh [YHWH] your Elohim for a sign. It can be anything you want"* (Isaiah 7:11 NOG).

But Ahaz spurned God and said that he would not ask, nor would he test the Lord. Isaiah said:

*"Listen now, descendants of David... Isn't it enough that you try the patience of mortals? Must you also try the patience of my Elohim? So Adonay himself will give you a sign: A virgin will become pregnant and give birth to a son, and she will name him Immanuel [God with us]. He will eat cheese and honey until he knows how to reject evil and choose good. Indeed, before the boy knows how to reject evil and choose good, the land of the two kings who terrify you will be deserted." (Isaiah 7:13–16)*

There have been several different interpretations of the "Immanuel" prophecy, but most of them point to it as a Messianic prophecy. It is essential to know that this message was sent to show that God would continue to be with His people, and would establish them if they believe in and honor Him. He would offer them safety and assurance as long as they trusted in Him. He would tabernacle with them and be their Immanuel throughout their life journey. And so He does with us.

## Lionel's Story

As a young boy, Lionel was intelligent and interested in school and other intellectual pursuits. He was always a deep thinker who did not accept things at face value. He grew up in a fatherless inner-city home, but with a mother who deeply loved the Lord and kept Lionel in the church.

Every Sunday, his mother would have him stay at home after church and read the Bible. Lionel wanted to go outside and play with his friends, but his mother was not having that. One Sunday afternoon, Lionel came upon a scripture in Exodus that said that the seventh day is the Sabbath. He went and looked at the calendar and noted that the seventh day was Saturday.

He promptly went to his mother's room and told her that Sunday was not the Sabbath or a holy day. The real Sabbath was Saturday. The ploy did not work, however, and Lionel still did not get to go outside. He put the scripture out of his mind.

When Lionel became a teenager, he succumbed to the influence of the gangs and streets. As he puts it, he was "up to no good in the hood." In the 1970s, the street gangs were rampant in New York. Gangs like the Black Spades, Peacemakers, Glory Stompers, Javelins, and the Social 7s dominated certain parts of the city and were very territorial. You could not cross into their territory without a "rumble."

There were drugs, stabbings, violence of various kinds, and general mayhem in these neighborhoods. Lionel found himself associating with one of the toughest gangs in the area at the time to protect himself and his family. If something happened to him or a member of his family, he felt that he needed backup; hence, he joined the toughest gang that he could find.

One time, Lionel recalled that he went up against a particular group of some local rivals and they had guns pointed directly at him. Before they could pull the triggers, a light surrounded him, and he just walked away. On several other occasions, some miraculous deliverance took place before harm could be done.

The very next day following one of these strange deliverances, he decided to go to his sister's apartment and tell her. His older sister, Sonia, was like a second mother to Lionel and they were very close. He said to her, "Something very strange happens every time it is time to go for a rumble, or when some crazy thing happens like someone is going to get stabbed or killed, I am not around. And whenever I am there, I seem to be supernaturally protected. The circumstances just seem to be maneuvering me elsewhere."

Sonia did not seem to pay any attention to what Lionel had just said to her. Instead, she totally changed the subject and told him that she had just joined a book club. "And look at the book I just bought— it's a Bible!" Lionel was almost offended. Didn't Sonia hear what he had just told her? His life had been on the line several times but spared.

Sonia then asked him to help her interpret a verse that she had read in Matthew 24:20, *"And pray that your flight will not be in the winter, or on the Sabbath."* What did that mean? What was the Sabbath, and why was it important enough that Jesus would tell His disciples to pray that their flight would not be on the Sabbath during the time of tribulation?

Lionel did not know the answer, but he decided to help his sister find out. He remembered the verses he had read as a child that had pointed to the seventh-day Sabbath.

Lionel began to look for the texts so that he could explain them to Sonia. He started to study, and the scriptures revealed God to him in a fresh, new way. Sonia was also researching and growing spiritually. She said that there must be a true church that is in harmony with the Scriptures, so she set out to find one. They had been keeping the Sabbath for six months and had not found a church. Lionel continued to study and learn more about God.

Eventually, Sonia found a church that emphasized the adherence to all ten of the commandments, and she began to attend that church. Lionel went to visit. It was the Ephesus Seventh-day Adventist Church. He heard the pastor, and Lionel felt the Spirit of God very heavily upon him. He felt as though God was speaking directly to him through the pastor. This challenged him to investigate the Scriptures even more. He began to look for God in every book, chapter, verse, and line of the Bible, noticing how God reveals Himself through His Word.

In studying the Bible, Lionel took note of how God manifests Himself through Providence and orchestrates the affairs of the lives of humanity. Then, Lionel had the realization that it was this same power that was protecting him, shielding him, and delivering him. Immanuel was always with Lionel, even when he did not acknowledge Him. All the puzzle pieces fell into place for him.

Lionel and his sister Sonia gave their hearts to Jesus and determined to follow Him for the rest of their lives. Lionel is a pastor in the Seventh-day Adventist Church and has faithfully served in that capacity for thirty years. He has never looked back. God has been with him throughout his journey. Lionel smiles as he thinks of his own middle name, "Emmanuel."

## Prayer:

*"**Immanuel**, God with us. How grateful I am that You are with me in every situation. No matter how dark my circumstances, You are there with me, to walk me through it. Oh, Immanuel, please show me the way in my current dilemma of _____. I need to know that You are with me every step of the way. Your presence is my assurance of victory. Thank you for being my guide through all of this. You are my King."*

"They will call on My name, and I will answer them. I will say, 'This is My people'; and each one will say, 'The LORD [YHWH] is my God.'"

—Zechariah 13:9

# – Chapter 10 –
# El Gibbor Milchamah:
# Mighty God of Battle
## (ehl-gib-bor mil-khah-mah)

*"Who is this King of glory? The Lᴏʀᴅ strong and*
*mighty, the Lᴏʀᴅ mighty in battle." (Psalm 24:8)*

I t has been noted that when the King of England returned to London
through Temple Bar, he was announced by a herald who demanded
entrance for the King: "Open the gate." From within a voice is heard,
"Who is there?" The herald answers, "The King of England!" The gate
is at once opened, and the king passes amidst the joyful acclamations
of his people. This is an ancient custom, and the allusion to it is in
this Psalm. [45]

Sometimes we think that God is soft. We often forget that He is
an amazing warrior, the omnipotent, victorious King. In Psalm 24:8,
the question is asked, *"Who is this King of glory?"* The answer is, *"The*
*Lᴏʀᴅ, strong and mighty, the Lᴏʀᴅ, mighty in battle"* (El Gibbor Milchamah). He is a God of victory and might. He is a God of power and
strength. A conquering King. He is the ruler of heaven and earth and
every living being on this planet and beyond.

We should never underestimate the strength of our God. He is the
One Who spoke the worlds into existence. He is the God Who led Israel
into battles and won, without challenge. He is the God Who delivers
His people miraculously and marvelously.

Consider what happened when the Lord led Israel out of Egypt. It is
one of the greatest God-led battles in all of history. You can read about
it in the book of Exodus. The Israelites had been enslaved by the Egyptians for 430 years. The Egyptians were cruel to them and made them
suffer undue hardship. Exodus 1:13–14 says:

*"So the Egyptians made the children of Israel serve with rigor.*
*And they made their lives bitter with hard bondage— in mortar,*

*in brick, and in all manner of service in the field. All their service in which they made them serve was with rigor."*

Life was so hard for the children of Israel. Over several generations, things got worse for them, not better. Rulers came and went, but the situation for the Israelites grew more and more difficult. Here is what it says in Exodus 2:23–25:

*"Now it happened in the process of time that the king of Egypt died. Then the children of Israel groaned because of the bondage, and they cried out; and their cry came up to God because of the bondage. So God heard their groaning, and God remembered His covenant with Abraham, with Isaac, and with Jacob. And God looked upon the children of Israel, and God acknowledged them."*

They cried out to the Lord for deliverance, and He heard them. He assured them of victory because it was He Who was fighting the battle for them. What He said to Moses about this is recorded in Exodus 6:6:

*"Therefore say to the children of Israel: I am the LORD [YHWH]; I will bring you out from under the burdens of the Egyptians, I will rescue you from their bondage, and I will redeem you with an outstretched arm and with great judgments."*

YHWH was letting His people know that He was going to deliver them. His acts of deliverance are meant to deepen the relationship that He has with His people, and to remind them that He is their God. Look at what He said in verse 7:

*"I will take you as My people, and I will be your God. Then you shall know that I am the LORD [YHWH] your God who brings you out from the burdens of the Egyptians."*

How did God deliver Israel from the Egyptians? He sent Moses and his brother, Aaron, to represent Him to the Pharaoh. Several times, Moses, as God's mouthpiece, told Pharaoh to let the people go, and Pharaoh refused. God poured ten plagues on the Egyptians[46]:

1) Water turned to blood

2) Frogs

3) Lice

4) Flies

5) Livestock diseased

6) Boils on man and beast

7) Hail

8) Locusts

9) Darkness

10) Death of firstborn

Finally, after the tenth plague, Pharaoh let the Israelites go. The people had been set free from the bondage of the Egyptians and were led by Moses, at God's command, into the wilderness. They were to camp between Migdol and the sea.

After reconsidering everything, Pharaoh and the Egyptians had a change of heart. In Exodus 14:5 we read:

*"Now it was told the king of Egypt that the people had fled and the heart of Pharaoh and his servants was turned against the people; and they said, 'Why have we done this, that we have let Israel go from serving us?'"*

They decided to go after the children of Israel and bring them back:

*"So the Egyptians pursued them, all the horses and chariots of Pharaoh, his horsemen and his army, and overtook them camping by the sea beside Pi Hahiroth, before Baal Zephon. And when Pharaoh drew near, the children of Israel lifted their eyes, and behold, the Egyptians marched after them. So they were very afraid and the children of Israel cried out to the LORD [YHWH]." (Exodus 14:9–10)*

Now, imagine that scene if you will. Moses and the children of Israel were encamped in the wilderness by the sea and pursued by Pharaoh and his army. The sea was in front of them, and this massive army was coming up behind them. They were geographically hemmed in. The people panicked. Where could they go? They were surrounded, with no escape. What could they do?

Moses said:

*"Do not be afraid. Stand still, and see the salvation of the LORD [YHWH], which He will accomplish for you today. For the Egyptians whom you see today, you shall see again no more forever. The LORD [YHWH] will fight for you, and you shall hold your peace." (Exodus 14:13–14)*

Is that beautiful, or what? I love the part that says, *"Stand still and see the salvation of the LORD."* There are times when we just must stand still and watch how the Lord intervenes on our behalf. The verse says that He will fight for us. What an amazing God.

The first thing that YHWH did was to put a cloud barrier between the children of Israel and the Egyptians:

*"And the Angel of God who went before the camp of Israel, moved and went behind them; and the pillar of cloud went from before them and stood behind them. So it came between the camp of the Egyptians and the camp of Israel. Thus it was a cloud and darkness to the one, and it gave light by night to the other, so that the one did not come near the other all that night." (Exodus 14:19–20)*

The Lord told Moses to lift his rod and stretch out his hand over the sea:

*"Then Moses stretched out his hand over the sea; and the LORD [YHWH] caused the sea to go back by a strong east wind all that night, and made the sea into dry land, and the waters were divided. So the children of Israel went into the midst of the sea on the dry ground, and the waters were a wall to them on their right hand and on their left. And the Egyptians pursued and went after them into the midst of the sea, all Pharaoh's horses, his chariots, and his horsemen." (Exodus 14:21–23)*

Can you just picture that? The Red Sea became two great walls of water all the way down to the bottom, which was dry land for the

Israelites to walk across. El Gibbor Milchamah, the Great Warrior, opened up the sea and led His people to safety.

Then there was the question of how to deal with the enemy. Here is what it says in Exodus 14:24–30:

> "Now it came to pass, in the morning watch, that the LORD looked down upon the army of the Egyptians through the pillar of fire and cloud, and He troubled the army of the Egyptians. And He took off their chariot wheels, so that they drove them with difficulty; and the Egyptians said 'Let us flee from the face of Israel, for the LORD fights for them against the Egyptians.'

> "Then the LORD said to Moses, 'Stretch out your hand over the sea, that the waters may come back upon the Egyptians, on their chariots, and on their horsemen.'

> "And Moses stretched out his hand over the sea; and when the morning appeared, the sea returned to its full depth, while the Egyptians were fleeing into it. So the LORD overthrew the Egyptians in the midst of the sea. Then the waters returned and covered the chariots, the horsemen, and all the army of Pharaoh that came into the sea after them. Not so much as one of them remained. But the children of Israel had walked on dry land in the midst of the sea, and the waters were a wall to them on their right hand and on their left.

> "So the LORD saved Israel that day out of the hand of the Egyptians, and Israel saw the Egyptians dead on the seashore."

Isn't that what He still does today? He receives us as His people and relieves us of the burdens that so heavily weigh us down.

And even more than the physical might, we cannot forget the spiritual power that El Gibbor Milchamah brings to bear. His Holy Spirit gives victory over sin in our lives. Satan is a defeated foe. Because of El Gibbor Milchamah, our God, Who is mighty in every battle, we too can defeat our giants—those strongholds or enemies that come up against us, both physically and spiritually.

In Isaiah 59:19 the Word of God says:

*"When the enemy comes in like a flood, the Spirit of the LORD will raise up a standard against him."*

We can feel secure in knowing that the battle is not ours; it is the Lord's. He will fight for us, and if God is for us, who can be against us? El Gibbor Milchamah, the Mighty God of Battle, has not lost a war yet, and never will.

## Phil's Story

Phil had been a professional paralegal for 15 years at the time. After transitioning to a new law firm, He found himself involved in a dispute that resulted in a devastating termination. He believed the dismissal to be unjust, groundless, and even possibly illegal. As time went on, and Phil had been unemployed for months, his finances were depleted, and he was in economic distress.

Phil considered suing his employer, but he had no resources to retain legal counsel. He was informally advised by people with legal knowledge not to pursue a lawsuit because he would probably never be able to win it.

Baked into their position, the employer refused all of Phil's efforts to settle the case out of court. They maintained that with such an imbalance of power and utility, Phil was low-hanging fruit for a comfortable victory for them; and from a human perspective, who could take reasonable issue with that? The employer lacked even a pretense of humility, oozing pride and assumed power from every pore.

Without resources, without legal counsel, and armed with nothing but faith and confidence in God's power, Phil believed that God was seeking to challenge his unjust termination. Phil knew that he, alone, was no match for his opponent. He was going up against the oldest, most experienced personal injury law firm in the large metropolitan city where he lived.

He filed a lawsuit "pro se" (i.e., by himself, without professional legal counsel). The defendant, on the other hand, retained a local, top-notch employment defense attorney with 32 years trial experience at that time. She had never lost a jury trial to date.

For three years, Phil had diligently been preparing for his trial, all while under deteriorating financial stress, intermittent periods of buckling faith, and at times an overwhelming sense of the daunting task of the ordeal ahead of him. This was a type of David versus

Goliath. How would he be able to stay afloat financially, prepare for the trial, and keep moving forward during one of the most challenging times of his life?

Unable to afford even the most basic necessities to put on a traditional trial, he forged ahead, confident that while a hopeless case in the sight of man, he and God constituted a majority.

It was one week before the trial. Phil had been diligently working on his computer, organizing all his information. Then, seemingly out of nowhere, his computer crashed, and he lost all that he had been preparing for his trial for the last three years. Phil put this greatest of setbacks in God's hands, reconstituted as much of his work as possible and steamed ahead to the first day of the trial.

On the morning of day one of the trial, Phil did not even have the money to pay for parking at the courthouse, so he asked a friend to drive him there. As he entered the courthouse, he found a quiet, unoccupied room and prayed this prayer: "Lord, I need strength, wisdom, and skill above that which I naturally have. Send me forth in the armor of heaven to prevail against this Goliath as it is according to Your will."

With that, Phil, with no trial experience of his own and declining trust in self, went into the courtroom and sat alone at the plaintiff's table before the judge. But he was far from alone. El Gibbor Milchamah, the Mighty God of Battle, was his unseen legal representative, and Phil imagined He was seated in the chair to his right. At the defense table were seated three of the most accomplished and decorated lawyers in the local Bar Association, with an aggregate trial experience of over 128 years.

Phil's opening statement at trial before a jury of 12 centered around the principles of the account of David and Goliath.

After a two-week, hard-fought, vigorous trial, the case went to the jury. After one day and a half, the court notified Phil that the jury had reached its verdict, and he appeared at the courthouse to receive it. The jurors entered the notably solemn courtroom. All stood reverently as the judge returned to her bench. They all sat down in great anticipation. The presiding juror handed the verdict to the bailiff, who handed the verdict to the judge.

The judge read the verdict—a verdict in favor of the Plaintiff, Phil, on ALL COUNTS. The jurors awarded Phil a six figure settlement.

As the verdict was read, one of Jeremiah's most reassuring questions came to Phil's mind:

*"Ah, Lord God! Behold, You have made the heavens and the earth by Your great power and outstretched arm. There is nothing too hard for You." ... Then the word of the LORD came to Jeremiah, saying, "Behold, I am the LORD, the God of all flesh. Is there anything too hard for Me?" (Jeremiah 32:17, 26–27)*

Glory be to God. El Gibbor Milchamah has given victory once again.

## Prayer:

*"**El Gibbor Milchamah,** You are mighty in battle. Right now, my biggest battle is _____, and I know that You will fight my battles for me. Step into my battle and give me the strength to endure. Please give me the wisdom that I need in order to gain the victory. With You, my victory is assured. Thank You, dear El Gibbor Milchamah."*

# Chapter 11

# YHWH Ropheka:
# The God Who Heals
# Adonai Ropheka (Spoken)
## (ah-do-nai ro-fe-ka)

*"He said, 'If you will listen carefully to Yahweh [YHWH] your Elohim and do what he considers right, if you pay attention to his commands and obey all his laws, I will never make you suffer any of the diseases I made the Egyptians suffer, because I am Yahweh [YHWH] Ropheka'" (Exodus 15:26 NOG)*

In Hebrew, the word "rophe" is a verb that means "to heal, cure, restore, or make whole."[47] We find the first allusion to this name of God in the book of Exodus. In Exodus chapter 14, we read the miraculous intervention by God in opening up the Red Sea and allowing the children of Israel to cross on dry land.

The Egyptians were in hot pursuit of them and attempted to follow them through the Red Sea pathway that God had made for His people. The problem was that it was not the path that the Egyptians were told to take. God had instructed Pharaoh to let His people go, to set them free, but Pharaoh's heart was hardened, and he decided to renege on his promise. Bad move. All of Pharaoh's army and chariots were destroyed as the Red Sea that had parted for the Israelites, closed, and drowned the Egyptians.

The Israelites watched as God's strong hand of deliverance, once again, intervened to bring them through a seemingly impossible situation. You would think that after having witnessed this mighty move of God, as well as having seen the ten plagues that had been placed upon Egypt (see Exodus chapters 7–12), that the Israelites would have trusted God, but that wasn't the case.

Just three days into the wilderness, there was no water. Then, when they got to Marah, the water was bitter and not drinkable. The people complained to Moses. Moses cried out to God, Who showed him a tree. God told Moses to cast the tree into the water, and when he did the water became sweet and drinkable. It was then that God told Moses that if the children of Israel would listen carefully and obey all of His commands and laws, He would put none of the diseases on them that He had put on the Egyptians, for He was YHWH Ropheka, the God Who Heals.

What great lessons we can draw from this part of the Israelites' journey. First of all, we may be quick to judge them for their disobedience. Yet how many times have we had some deep experience with the Lord only to fall back into sin shortly thereafter? How many times have we forgotten the ways that He has delivered us from bad situations? How many times have we demonstrated a lack of faith and trust in the God Who has never left or forsaken us?

Secondly, we need to be reminded that He is the God Who heals us, but there are conditions. He expects us to obey His laws of health and not to abuse our bodies by disregarding His health laws of nutrition, exercise, water, sunshine, fresh air, rest, and trust in God.[48] We can lead healthy lives if we obey God's laws of health. Why should God heal you from lung cancer, for example, if you are going to continue to smoke cigarettes?

Of course, every illness is not due to breaking God's health laws. Some illnesses occur from out of the blue and are just the result of the sinful world in which we live. It is great to know that we can trust God, our Adonai Ropheka, under all circumstances, for He is the God Who heals.

Just ask Chris:

## Chris's Story

"This pregnancy is different from my previous one," Chris thought. Indeed, it was. She was having health issues that she had never before experienced, such as extreme fatigue and near fainting. Within two weeks of her birth, little Audrey developed some unfamiliar looking skin rashes. Even the pediatrician was baffled. He scoured his medical books to find out what it was, but to no avail.

This went on for months. Chris was breastfeeding Audrey, so she was very careful with her own diet, just in case it was something that she was ingesting that was causing the rashes.

After she was weaned, Audrey's health worsened. If she showed symptoms of having something as seemingly harmless as a common cold, within two or three hours it would develop into acute bronchitis, or pneumonia. Chris tried natural remedies, and nothing seemed to work. Audrey was practically quarantined. The doctor suggested that she not be exposed to other people or even around people at church.

Eventually, he prescribed antibiotics and a home nebulizer (a small machine that turns liquid medicine into a mist that flows directly into the lungs). If Audrey began to sneeze, she was to receive the antibiotics. Whenever Audrey caught a cold, her lungs would fill up with mucus. She was tested for cystic fibrosis, and although she was not diagnosed with that disease, for much of her childhood she had to be hospitalized.

When Audrey was about nine, she caught a cold and her lungs filled up with mucus. Her breathing was labored. Chris rushed her to the emergency room, where the physicians and nurses worked for hours to relieve her symptoms, but to no avail. They decided to airlift Audrey to the children's hospital in St. Louis, Missouri. Chris was not allowed to fly with her, so she had to drive the two and a half hours to the St. Louis Children's Hospital. Chris was praying constantly for God's intervention.

When Chris arrived at the hospital, she discovered that Audrey had been diagnosed with influenza A. The hospital staff worked tirelessly to help little Audrey, but she was in trouble and needed to go to the intensive care unit. There was no room at that hospital, so she had to be taken by ambulance to St. John's Hospital.

Again, Chris and Audrey were separated, because Chris was not able to ride in the ambulance with her. When Chris arrived at St. John's, she went to the intensive care unit and saw her baby girl desperately struggling to breathe. Chris took her in her arms. As she was holding her, a specialist came in to check her. He was not there but five minutes or so, when Audrey pushed out the words, 'Help me," and she completely stopped breathing in Chris's arms. She suffered complete respiratory failure. In most cases, this meant certain death. The staff removed Chris from the room as they scrambled to put Audrey on life support.

The physician told Chris that they were going to have to push eighty pounds of pressure into Audrey's lungs, which were only capable of twenty pounds. They were expecting her little lungs to burst from the pressure, but they would do all that they could. Audrey was being kept mechanically alive on a breathing machine.

The doctor suggested that Chris find a place locally to stay. He said that if Audrey stayed alive on the ventilator, it would still be months before she could be well enough to go home.

Chris contacted friends, family, and the word went out about little Audrey. All around the country, folks were praying for her. Chris even contacted 3ABN Radio, and requests for prayer were all over the airwaves. Then, Chris remembered James 5:14:

> *"Is anyone among you sick? Let him call for the elders of the church, and let them pray over him, anointing him with oil in the name of the Lord."*

By now, it was mid-week. Chris invited Pastor Kenny Shelton and one of his associates to anoint Audrey. Approximately thirty minutes after the anointing prayer service, all the alarms of the ventilator began to sound. Chris did not understand what was happening and began to struggle with God through her tears, as the staff rushed her away from Audrey once again. Chris knew that Audrey was not breathing on her own. "Why are all of these alarms ringing?" she wondered. "Are my baby's organs shutting down?"

Finally, a nurse came in and explained what was going on. Audrey's lungs had begun to function properly after the anointing. When the lungs were operating independently they were no longer in sync with the ventilator, thus causing the alarms to sound.

Adonai Ropheka is a healing God. He heard Chris's prayers and the many who joined her in petitioning Him for little Audrey's healing. What an awesome God we serve.

## Prayer (For You):

*"Dear **Adonai Ropheka**, I need a touch from You, the Divine Physician. Earthly physicians may give me a diagnosis, but You are the One that I look to for guidance. Show me how to live according to Your ways and lead me to the right physicians who will guide me according to Your will for me. Help me to trust You for the outcome, no matter what that might be. I pray for healing, but that might not be what You have in mind for me right now. Let Your will be done. Give me the strength to trust in You regardless of the outcome. In the worthy name of Yeshua (Jesus), I pray, Amen."*

## Prayer (For Others):

*"Dear **Adonai Ropheka**, _____ really needs to be healed. You have invited us to come to You when we have a need, so that is what I am doing right now. I trust You, Lord. You know everything about _____. You know how this illness began, and You know when it will end. Please, Father, in the name of Yeshua (Jesus), I beg You to intervene in this situation and heal _____. I trust that You will do what is best, and that when You heal, You heal completely. Thank You, oh Adonai Ropheka, for Your complete healing and restoration. In the worthy name of Yeshua (Jesus), I pray, Amen."*

> "And blessed be His glorious name forever! And let the whole earth be filled with His glory. Amen and Amen."
>
> —Psalm 72:19

# – Chapter 12 –
# El Yeshuati:
# God of My Salvation
## *(ehl-ye-shoo-ah-tee)*

*"Behold, God is my salvation. I will trust and not be
afraid; for Yah, the LORD, is my strength and song;
He has also become my salvation." (Isaiah 12:2)*

The word *salvation* has been used in many ways and multiple times.
What does it really mean? "In Christianity, salvation (also called
deliverance or redemption) is the 'saving [of] human beings from
death and separation from God' by Christ's death and resurrection,
and the justification following this salvation." [49]

It is Isaiah who refers to God as El Yeshuati, or "The God of My
Salvation." Yeshuati is a variant of Yeshua or transliterated into Greek,
"Jesus," which means "Yah is salvation." In Isaiah's time, his people, the
Israelites, had been taken into captivity by the Babylonians. Isaiah was
called by God to be a prophet or messenger to them.

Through Isaiah, God sent messages of hope and judgment to His
people and the surrounding nations. In Isaiah chapter 12, we find a
hymn of praise for YAH (a derivative of "YHWH"), the LORD, in His
deliverance of His people. However, it is more than that. It is an expres-
sion of appreciation for the rescue by God, as demonstrated in salvation.

In this same chapter, verse 3, we read:

*"Therefore with joy you will draw water from the wells of salvation."*

The Feast of Tabernacles was a yearly convocation that was held
in the fall of the year and was eight days long. The first and last days
were the most sacred. During the Feast of Tabernacles, all the people
would gather in Jerusalem and live in "booths." Even the residents of
Jerusalem would leave their homes and live in these little huts made
from branches and wood.

These booths represented the way the children of Israel lived while in the wilderness after their exodus from Egypt. In fact, one of the purposes of the Feast of Tabernacles was to remember God's miraculous provision for His people during their forty years of wandering through the wilderness. He provided their daily food (in the form of manna), their shoes and clothes did not wear out, and He gave them water from a rock. It is this very provision of water that also is a symbol of the provision of the Living Water provided by El Yeshuati.

There was a ritual performed by the priest on each day of the feast. In the morning, he, followed by a processional of the people, would take a large golden bowl down to the Pool of Siloam. There, he would fill it with water, and place the bowl on the top of his head before ascending the stairs back to the Temple. "As the procession entered the Court of the Temple, the trumpets sounded and all the throngs of people sang, 'With joy shall ye draw water out of the wells of salvation.'"[50] This statement was both a look back into history as well as a prophecy.

In John chapter 7, we read that Jesus went to the Feast of Tabernacles, and on the last day, the most sacred day of the feast, He stood up and cried out:

> *"If anyone thirsts, let him come to Me and drink. He who believes in Me as the Scripture has said, out of his heart will flow rivers of living water." (John 7:37–38)*

The Feast of Tabernacles pointed to Jesus as the One from Whom we can obtain the water of eternal life for our thirsty souls. To those who believe in Him, Jesus, our Yeshuati, will send the Holy Spirit. He will guide us into all truth and satisfy our deepest thirst:

> *"And the Spirit and the bride say, 'Come!' And let him who hears say, 'Come!' And let him who thirsts come. Whoever desires, let him take the water of life freely." (Revelation 22:17)*

> *"For I will pour water on him who is thirsty, and floods on the dry ground; I will pour My Spirit on your descendants, and My blessing on your offspring." (Isaiah 44:3)*

Salvation is a Divine act (Psalm 3:8) which cannot be implemented by a human being. It is an act of God Himself that transforms the character of the saved. As believers, we are delivered from darkness (2 Corinthians 4:6), saved from the power and condemnation of sin, and offered eternal life through the sacrifice of our Lord Jesus Christ.

We do not need to fear anything, for the God of our salvation, El Yeshuati, is our defense and our strength. We only need to trust and obey Him. Our outcome is assured.

Look at how El Yeshuati manifested Himself in Bruce's life:

## Bruce's story

Bruce remembers vividly the event that caused him to become a survivor rather than a dependent. It broke the trust he had in his family and did not allow him to trust his fellow man and, unintentionally, his Savior.

When Bruce was about seven or eight years old, his family planned a special day to go to his grandfather's gold mine. Bruce was very excited about it and looked forward to the trip. It was a real treat for him to get to hang out with his older cousins.

On the way up, they stopped at a store next to a fire station. While waiting for their grandpa to come out of the store, one of the cousins went into the fire station and stole some girly magazines. After arriving up in the mountains, they all took off to explore and have fun. They were by a steep bank that had something shiny that looked like a 50-cent piece way over the edge. Bruce's cousins and brothers encouraged him to go get it. Wanting to please, he scrambled down the bank as quickly as he could, only to find that it was a bottle cap.

When he reported back that it was only a bottle cap, they started throwing rocks down at him to keep him from witnessing what was planned with the girly magazines. When the rocks stopped coming, Bruce went back up the bank onto the dusty road only to discover that they were gone, and he was all alone. The pain of being hit by the rocks was forgotten when he found that he was all alone and lost.

Bruce had a real meltdown and then decided to find his grandpa. Somehow, he followed his cousins' tracks and found where his grandpa's mine was. He went into the shaft a little way to see if he could find his grandpa, but it was so dark and scary that he decided to go back outside and play by himself. From that day until many years afterward, Bruce had difficulty trusting anyone, including God.

Bruce started experimenting with alcohol in the eighth grade, and the buzz he received from drinking was something he had never experienced before. It seemed fun and harmless. The drinking continued uninterrupted until his junior year in high school, where he was attending a Christian academy.

One evening at about 8 p.m., he received a phone call from his mother. She told him that his brother, Calvin, age 19, was killed that day in a truck accident. She said that his dying words were to Jesus—that he did not want to die, and that he wanted to go to heaven with Jesus. God heard Calvin's prayer that day, but did what was best, and allowed Calvin to go to sleep in Him.

That call jolted Bruce profoundly and made him realize that life can be short. God knew that Bruce was leading a life apart from Him. He was doing what he wanted to make himself feel good. Bruce knew that he was not on his way to heaven, and so badly wanted to see his brother again, that he prayed and asked for forgiveness. He experienced another answer to prayer.

Bruce turned to Jesus instead of his vices for the feeling, although the peace he found did not give him the same feelings that alcohol and marijuana had given him. He was content and happy, even joyful, knowing that he was doing what he could to ensure a reunion with his brother. He wanted to witness what the power of prayer was doing for his life and the lives of others. The rest of his high school years were filled with fun and joy, except for the pain he felt when he remembered his brother.

It was during the last of his teenage years that Bruce was encouraged by an older cousin to pursue alcohol and sexual relationships with women as his focus in life. He did not have intimate conversations with his parents, so he was devoid of direction. Although he had gotten baptized when he was twelve, it was a mere formality to Bruce. Christianity was very behaviorally orientated rather than relationship-driven in his life.

After graduation from high school, Bruce began working in the family business, crushing cars in a territory that covered seven western states. He lived in motels and ate in restaurants. The transition from school into an adult working life was a challenge. The problems started happening rather quickly as he no longer made the time for worship and time with Jesus. He also stopped listening to Christian music. Bruce began to listen to the rock-n-roll of the '60s and '70s and soon found himself living the life of the songs he was listening to. Drinking and drug use went on daily for about 15 years.

One day Bruce came home from work and found a note taped to the front door telling him that his son Brian was across the street at the neighbors, and his wife and two stepdaughters were gone and would not be returning.

Bruce went to get Brian and found him in a fetal position in the corner of the neighbor's house. They said that he had been that way for over three hours. Bruce picked him up and took him home to find an almost empty house. Their beds and clothes were there as well as a couch and a drawer full of unpaid bills that were three months overdue.

He held Brian for over two hours trying to comfort him, acutely feeling the pain he had caused by his lifestyle of drinking and drugs. Bruce was a high-functioning addict. He held down a good job, made good money, but spent most of it on his self-indulgent habits.

Brian finally relaxed after hours of reassurance. Bruce let him know that it was not his fault that the family had left and that he would not leave him. After getting Brian into bed, Bruce proceeded to get drunk and high, listening to the voices of shame and failure that he was never going to overcome his addictions.

Thinking Brian would be better off if he were dead, Bruce loaded his pistol and held it to his head. He was about to squeeze the trigger, when he heard a voice. It was a voice of encouragement saying, "I love you, don't do this, I'm not finished with you yet." Bruce responded, "Oh, yeah, if You love me so much, why can't I overcome my addictions? I have asked You multiple times to help me, but I end up going back to them." Bruce added, "OK, pal, but if it doesn't work out, I will come back here and finish the job I started tonight."

Bruce decided to follow Jesus and rely on His power to help him overcome Satan's grip on his life. He knew that he needed a Savior.

That night marked a turning point in Bruce's relationship with God. Bruce threw away his drugs and poured his alcohol down the drain. He asked Jesus to help him to overcome and to heal Brian from his pain. Jesus is faithful. He answered Bruce's prayer that night. Jesus is El Yeshuati, the God of My Salvation. There is no situation confronting you that He has not evaluated and measured. Over thirty-two years ago, El Yeshuati saved Bruce from a life of self-destruction and legalism. And He can do the same for you.

## Prayer:

"Dear **El Yeshuati,** You are the God of My Salvation. You are The One Who can deliver me from my most self-destructive habits. You bring me into a real relationship with You, not one that is merely rule-driven, or performance motivated. You will send the Holy Spirit into my life to provide me with the Living Water so that I will never thirst again. Thank you for knowing me for who I am and loving me just the same. Help me to love and seek You with all of my heart."

# – Chapter 13 –
# El Elyon:
# Most High God
## *(ehl-ehl-yohn)*

*"I call to Elohim Elyon, to El who does
everything for me." (Psalm 57:2 NOG)*

Our first introduction to the title, "El Elyon" is in Genesis 14. The
chapter begins by describing that a war had broken out: four
kings against five. Lot, Abram's nephew, was taken captive. One
of the captives escaped and told Abram that Lot and his possessions
were taken.

When Abram heard this, he quickly armed three hundred eighteen
of his trained servants and went in pursuit of Lot's captors. The Bible
says that Abram:

*"...divided his forces against them by night, and he and his
servants attacked them and pursued them as far as Hobah, which
is north of Damascus. So he brought back all the goods, and also
brought back his brother Lot and his goods, as well as the women
and the people" (Genesis 14:15–16)* [51]

What a rescue mission. Abram was a valiant fighter, who had the
El Elyon, The Most High God on his side. Upon his return, the King
of Sodom went out to meet Abram; then Melchizedek, King of Salem
brought out bread and wine. He was a priest of El Elyon. He blessed
Abram and said:

*"Blessed is Abram by El Elyon, maker of heaven and earth.
Blessed is El Elyon, who has handed your enemies over to you."
(Genesis 14:18–20 NOG)*

This was Abram's first introduction to this title of God. The King
of Sodom told Abram to take all the spoils from the rescue and just

return the people. Abram refused. He raised his hand and swore before El Elyon, Maker of heaven and earth, that he would not take even a thread or a sandal strap. He never wanted them to be able to say that they made him rich. The only thing he took was the food that his men ate. Abram suggested that his allies could take their share, but he was not taking any of it.

The "El" in the Hebrew denotes "God," "Power" or "Might." [52] It is the same word as in El Shaddai, or as the root of Elohim. [53] Elyon in Hebrew means "Most High." [54] It applies to the highest of its type. In other words, there is none higher. Abram had just fought in a war against earthly kings. He was being entertained by the King of Sodom (King Bera) and Melchizedek, King of Salem and priest. Abram was assisted, though, by El Elyon, the Most High: The King of Kings, above Who there is no other.

Another interesting encounter with the name El Elyon is in Daniel chapter 4. King Nebuchadnezzar of Babylon was a heathen king who had attacked Jerusalem in 605 BC. Some young noblemen from prominent Jewish families were taken captive by his armies.

He renamed some of his Hebrew captives after his gods. Daniel, in Hebrew, means "God is My Judge." [55] Nebuchadnezzar renamed him, "Belteshazzar," which means "May Bel Protect His Life". [56]

Nebuchadnezzar took various items from the Temple of God in Jerusalem and put them into the temple of his god. Nebuchadnezzar felt invincible and was steeped in Babylonian culture.

One night, Nebuchadnezzar had a dream that troubled him. He called in the magicians, astrologers, and the soothsayers in his administration, but no one could tell him what the dream meant. No one, that is, except Daniel. Here is Nebuchadnezzar's dream: [57]

*"These were the visions of my head while on my bed: I was looking, and behold, a tree in the midst of the earth, and its height was great. The tree grew and became strong; its height reached to the heavens, and it could be seen to the ends of all the earth. Its leaves were lovely, its fruit abundant, and in it was food for all. The beasts of the field found shade under it, the birds of the heavens dwelt in its branches, and all flesh was fed from it.*

*"I saw in the visions of my head while on my bed, and there was a watcher, a holy one, coming down from heaven. He cried aloud*

*and said thus: 'Chop down the tree and cut off its branches, strip off its leaves and scatter its fruit. Let the beasts get out from under it, and the birds from its branches.*

*" 'Nevertheless leave the stump and roots in the earth, bound with a band of iron and bronze, in the tender grass of the field. Let it be wet with the dew of heaven, and let him graze with the beasts on the grass of the earth. Let his heart be changed from that of a man, let him be given the heart of a beast, and let seven times pass over him.*

*" 'This decision is by the decree of the watchers, and the sentence by the word of the holy ones, In order that the living may know that the Most High [El Elyon] rules in the kingdom of men, gives it to whomever He will, and sets over it the lowest of men.'*

*"This dream I, King Nebuchadnezzar, have seen. Now you, Belteshazzar, declare its interpretation, since all the wise men of my kingdom are not able to make known to me the interpretation; but you are able, for the Spirit of the Holy God is in you."* (Daniel 4:10–26)

Daniel was troubled by the interpretation of the dream, and did not want to tell Nebuchadnezzar what it meant, but the King insisted. Daniel said, in verses 20–27:

*"The tree that you saw, which grew and became strong, whose height reached to the heavens and which could be seen by all the earth, whose leaves were lovely and its fruit abundant, in which was food for all, under which the beasts of the field dwelt, and in whose branches the birds of the heaven had their home— it is you, O king, who have grown and become strong; for your greatness has grown and reaches to the heavens, and your dominion to the end of the earth.*

*"And inasmuch as the king saw a watcher, a holy one, coming down from heaven and saying, 'Chop down the tree and destroy it, but leave its stump and roots in the earth, bound with a band of iron and bronze in the tender grass of the field; let it be wet*

*with the dew of heaven, and let him graze with the beasts of the field, till seven times pass over him'; this is the interpretation, O king, and this is the decree of the Most High [El Elyon] which has come upon my lord the king: they shall drive you from men, your dwelling shall be with the beasts of the field, and they shall make you eat grass like oxen. They shall wet you with the dew of heaven, and seven times shall pass over you, till you know that the Most High [El Elyon] rules in the kingdom of men, and gives it to whomever He chooses.*

*"And inasmuch as they gave the command to leave the stump and roots of the tree, your kingdom shall be assured to you, after you come to know that Heaven rules. Therefore, O king, let my advice be acceptable to you; break off your sins by being righteous, and your iniquities by showing mercy to the poor. Perhaps there may be a lengthening of your prosperity."*

This is a fascinating dream and interpretation. To absorb its importance, one must understand the character and history of Nebuchadnezzar. [58] He was the son of Nabopolassar, founder of the Chaldean empire. Nebuchadnezzar was his firstborn child (born 630 BC), and his heir to the throne.

Early on, Nabopolassar began to groom Nebuchadnezzar to be a warrior and a ruler. According to tradition, Nebuchadnezzar began his military career as a young man, and was a military administrator around the age of 20. Nebuchadnezzar was also caught up in the pagan religions of his day. The chief Babylonian god at the time was Marduk, and Nebuchadnezzar, as a youth, worked as a laborer in the restoration of the temple of Marduk.

Within three weeks after his father's death, Nebuchadnezzar ascended the throne as king. He continued his military strategies and acquisitions, and in 597 BC, attacked Judah and captured Jerusalem. His was a regime of territorial expansion, claiming the right of universal kingship by his god, Marduk.

History records Nebuchadnezzar's primary activity outside of military conquests was the rebuilding of Babylon.

He completed and extended fortifications begun by his father, built a great moat and a new outer defense wall, paved the ceremonial Processional Way with limestone, rebuilt and embellished the principle temples, and cut canals. This he did not only for his own glorification, but also in honor of his gods. He claimed to be 'the one who set in the mouth of the people reverence for the great gods' and disparaged predecessors who had built palaces elsewhere than at Babylon and had only journeyed there for the New Year Feast. [59]

Nebuchadnezzar was bold, headstrong, and arrogant. In fact, Daniel, as he interpreted the King's dream told him (verses 20–22) that he (Nebuchadnezzar) was the "tree that grew and became strong, whose height reached to the heavens and which could be seen by all the earth."

*"It is you, O king," Daniel said, "who have grown and become strong; for your greatness has grown and reaches to the heavens, and your dominion to the end of the earth."*

The bad news was that El Elyon, the Most High God, had decreed that Nebuchadnezzar would be driven from the palace and would live like a beast for seven years, until he knew that the Most High: *"...rules in the kingdom of men, and gives it to whomever He chooses" (Daniel 4:25).*

God, in His mercy, was not permanently removing Nebuchadnezzar from his throne, but just long enough to teach him who the real Ruler was. Daniel pleaded with Nebuchadnezzar to break off his sins by being righteous, and his iniquities by showing mercy to the poor. He said that perhaps his prosperity could be lengthened a bit if he were to forsake his sins.

And then it happened. One year later, Nebuchadnezzar was walking around in the royal palace of Babylon and was feeling conceited. He said (verse 30), *"Is not this great Babylon that I have built for a royal dwelling by my mighty power and for the honor of my majesty?"*

Then the Bible states that:

*"While the word was still in the king's mouth, a voice fell from heaven: 'King Nebuchadnezzar, to you it is spoken: the kingdom departed from you! And they shall drive you from men, and your dwelling shall be with the beasts of the field. They shall make you eat grass like oxen; and seven times shall pass over you, until you*

*know that the Most High [El Elyon] rules in the kingdom of men, and gives it to whomever He chooses.'" (Daniel 4:30–32)*

The great warrior and king, Nebuchadnezzar, was humbled by the Most High God.

It is the Most High Who determines who reigns and rules on earth. It is El Elyon who has no competition, for there is none greater than He. Yet, He is merciful. After the seven years were ended, He restored Nebuchadnezzar back to his throne. This time, Nebuchadnezzar acknowledged the Most High God, El Elyon. Nebuchadnezzar said:

*"And at the end of the time, I Nebuchadnezzar, lifted my eyes to heaven, and my understanding returned to me; and I blessed the Most High and praised and honored Him who lives forever. For His dominion is an everlasting dominion, and His kingdom is from generation to generation. All the inhabitants of the earth are reputed as nothing; He does according to His will in the army of heaven and among the inhabitants of the earth. No one can restrain His hand or say to Him,'What have You done?'*

*"At the same time my reason returned to me, and for the glory of my kingdom, my honor and splendor returned to me. My counselors and nobles resorted to me, I was restored to my kingdom, and excellent majesty was added to me. Now I, Nebuchadnezzar, praise and extol and honor the King of heaven, all of whose works are truth, and His ways justice. And those who walk in pride He is able to put down." (Daniel 4:34–37)*

El Elyon, the Most High God, is ever merciful. He sits on high and is aware of everything about us. He is ever seeking to show His kindness and love. Just ask Wendell:

## Wendell's Story

Wendell only has fragments of memories of his early years. Trauma can do that to you sometimes. He was born in 1943. His Dad was a United States Navy pilot who was killed when his plane was shot down during World War II. After his death, Wendell's mother met and married a man who drank heavily and did not want any children.

One of Wendell's first memories was that of being left on the side of the road when he was about two or three years old. He was found and taken to a family that owned a farm. He stayed there for a year or so, and then was adopted by a very kind couple, Herbert and Emma. They lived on a dairy farm with orchards of fruit trees and a huge garden of fruits and vegetables.

The couple later adopted another young boy named Jack, whose parents had been killed in a fire. Wendell and Jack were typical siblings who loved each other but fought from time to time. Their home was stable and happy.

It was during his school years that Wendell fell in love with percussion instruments, particularly the marimba and all of the drums. He began to play with different bands, first in school, and then outside of it. After he left high school, and throughout college, Wendell began to experiment with different addictive substances. He started playing with some well-known groups and had access to all kinds of drugs. His drugs of choice: marijuana, heroin and cocaine.

While on the road with various groups, Wendell became more and more hooked on drugs. That lead him into some sketchy relationships. Eventually, he married three times, each time to a woman he had met during one of the concerts at which he happened to be playing.

The first marriage yielded two boys and the second marriage, a boy and a girl. The third marriage brought another boy and girl. None of the marriages worked out. Although Wendell did not stay married to any of his wives, he still sent money to them to support his children.

Wendell continued to use drugs and to spiral downward. He got so depressed from the futility of it all, that he even attempted suicide. He was so discouraged. Was there more to life than this? How could he have fallen so low? There were times when Wendell just felt hopeless.

El Elyon, the Most High God, had been watching Wendell and had sent spiritual people into his life path. A kind woman named Dorothy, the mother of a musician friend of Wendell's, invited him to attend church with her during some of his school breaks. Also, a friend named Jason invited Wendell to go to his Pentecostal church; in 1997, Wendell was baptized into his church, but felt that he was not receiving sufficient Bible knowledge.

Dorothy gave Wendell a study Bible as a college graduation gift, and he really valued it. He got a job on a cruise ship as a percussionist, and while others on the ship were partying, Wendell would go to his room to study his Bible. He was searching for answers to some of his deepest questions.

About a year following the cruise ship job, Wendell took a position as a limousine driver. He started attending a non-denominational church where they spoke in tongues. He worked nights as a limousine driver, so he always got home in the early hours of the morning. Then he would have a cigar, drink some beer or wine and watch television.

One time, while flipping through the channels, he heard a man talking about speaking in tongues, so he stopped and listened to him. The man cleared up Wendell's misunderstanding of tongues. He shared what the true gift of tongues really was. Wendell later learned that he was watching 3ABN. He became very interested and could not wait to get home every morning to turn to that channel.

From watching 3ABN, Wendell learned about new ways of worship. He learned that the Sabbath is Saturday, not Sunday. One Saturday, Wendell and his daughter-in-law went to visit a local Seventh-day Adventist Church. They were greeted by a gentleman with a big smile of welcome on his face. Wendell began to regularly attend this church. Then he began Bible studies and was baptized in 2005. Now he is a deacon in his church, feeding the homeless, and sharing Jesus with anyone who will listen. He has never had such joy.

Wendell looks back over his life, and he sees how El Elyon, the Most High God, was watching over him. He says, "After putting my life in the hands of my best friend and Savior, Jesus Christ, I look back on my life from the beginning to the present time; I understand how He was with me, not letting me die through all of my destructive life of drug abuse, very bad associates, attempting suicide, and treating people selfishly."

Yes, El Elyon was protecting Wendell at his darkest times: through his drug addictions and promiscuity. The Most High was there watching over him when he attempted suicide, and when a mobster held a gun to his chest, threatening to kill him. El Elyon was there, sitting high, and looking low.

El Elyon is also watching over you. Imagine this: His attention never falters. You are on His radar 24/7. He is the Most High God and He loves and watches over YOU.

## Prayer:

*"**Dear El Elyon,** Most High God, there is no one like You. You know everything about me, Your care never waivers, and You always have my back. Sometimes I may forget Who You are— the SUPREME GOD OF THE UNIVERSE. There is no one who compares to You, and You are my Friend. Thank You so much for Your loving care and kindness. Help me not to take You for granted, but to remember that You are in charge of everything. So, when chaos is going on all around me, I can exhale and trust that You will work all situations out for my good. Thank You, El Elyon."*

"The name of the LORD is a strong tower; the righteous run to it and are safe"

—Proverbs 18:10

# – Chapter 14 –
# Elohim Ahavah: God of Love
## *(ehl-o-heem ah-hah-vah)*

*"The LORD has appeared of old to me, saying: 'Yes, I have loved you with an everlasting love; Therefore with lovingkindness I have drawn you.'"* (Jeremiah 31:3)

Sharon picked up her keys to go home. It was daybreak, and she needed to run to her house to change clothes before heading to work. How did she end up being out all night? She felt such emptiness. Why didn't Nick feel for her the way she felt about him? Yes, they had had some enjoyable times together, but she could tell that he was just using her. "Why doesn't he love me?" she wondered.

Rob decided that he had had enough. Susan was a gold digger, and he knew it. He had bought her the best that money could buy, yet she always wanted more. She was not interested in spending quality time with him; she just wanted his money. Her excuses were getting old. He felt manipulated and played for a fool once again.

Have you ever just wanted to be loved for who you are? Have you wished that you were enough and that the things about you that you don't even find attractive would be precious to someone else? Elohim Ahavah, the God of Love, adores you. Yes, YOU, with all of your physical, emotional, and spiritual imperfections. He has a heart for you and longs to deepen His relationship with you.

What do you do when you are in love? First, you spend time together. I remember when my husband, Danny, and I first met. I came to 3ABN for an interview on a book that I had written, and Danny was my interviewer on the 3ABN Today program. He was charming and funny. I instantly liked him.

From that first day on (except for a few "hiccups" in-between), we would talk. We talked for hours, getting to know each other. I lived in Dallas at the time, and he lived in Illinois, but the distance didn't stop us from burning up those telephone wires. We talked about our child-hood, our kids, our relationships, our ministries and careers.

Danny has a way of making you feel exceptional. I fell in love with him very soon after meeting him. In fact, for me, I think it was almost love at first sight. The more time that I spent talking with him, the more I loved him. The more of himself that he revealed to me, the more I loved him.

With our God, the more we learn about Him and His character, the more we should appreciate and love Him. However, the difference between us and God is that He loved us before we were born or conceived:

*"Before I formed you in the womb I knew you; Before you were born I sanctified you." (Jeremiah 1:5)*

Before we even have come to know God, He is in love with us.

Not only did He know and love you before you were formed and conceived, but He also made a plan of salvation for you before the world was even created. It was the greatest, most profound demonstration of His love possible. God gave us His only begotten Son:

*"For God so loved the world that He gave His only begotten Son, that whoever believes in Him should not perish but have everlasting life." (John 3:16)*

*"But God demonstrates His own love toward us, in that while we were still sinners, Christ died for us." (Romans 5:8)*

He offered us, as sinners, a way to be with Him forever. And in 1 John 3:1–2 we read:

*"Behold what manner of love the Father has bestowed on us, that we should be called children of God! ... Beloved, now we are children of God; and it has not yet been revealed what we shall be, but we know that when He is revealed, we shall be like Him, for we shall see Him as He is."*

You should never doubt God's love for you. Elohim Ahavah, the God of Love, will never leave you nor forsake you. He loves you just as you are, with all your flaws and hangups. He wants to help you to conform to the image of His Son, and to prepare you for a life with Him forever.

Ann knew what it was like to need love:

## Ann's Story

Ann had a tough exterior, and everyone who met her knew not to mess with her. That was just the way she wanted it. After all, she had had to fight for everything that she'd ever had. She was determined not to let her real personality show to anyone. They would surely interpret it as a weakness.

Ann does not remember much about her early years. That is probably because she was so hurt from her childhood that she repressed a lot of what happened to her. Ann grew up in a dysfunctional environment. She was raised in multiple foster homes.

Ann's biological mother, Lynn, was about 14 when she had her, and 16 or 17 when she had Ann's little brother. Lynn was a tough young girl, herself, and gave her own mother a hard time. Ann never knew her father, but by her light eyes and fair skin, she thought she might have been biracial.

One day, when Ann was about three years old, something happened that changed her life forever. A policeman came to take her mother away. Lynn was a minor, had been impregnated twice, and was rebellious, so she was being sent to a home for wayward minors. When the policeman came to the house, Ann's mother and little Ann were outside. Ann was a slight distance away from her mother and began to move toward her. Lynn said, "I can't leave my baby!" Ann started heading over to her mother, but Lynn pushed past her and headed towards the house to see her baby boy one more time. The pain that Ann felt from that rejection never left her.

She didn't see her mother again for another 16 years. Ann was in and out of foster homes, where she did not receive love and caring. It was not until the last foster home that she even felt as though someone cared about her. By then, Ann was a teenager, so a lot of the emotional damage had already been done. She acted as though love for her did not matter.

Ann became very street smart as she grew up and had a gift for being able to read people's agendas. She also found herself pregnant at an early age and became a mother when she was eighteen. She had a set of twin boys. Once Ann became a mother, her focus was on her and her children. She was determined to offer them a better life than she had growing up.

Ann got involved in community enhancement and received housing through a unique government program. In time, she had seven children. Her twins were grown and out of the house, and she had four girls and one boy at home. Although there was not much money to go around, Ann made sure that her children were clean and well educated. She was a fighter and would stand up to any perceived injustice. As a result, people generally stayed away from her.

Ann had a small group of acquaintances with whom she played cards and gambled for extra money. With few exceptions, her relationships were generally superficial. One day a friend from work told Ann about Jesus. Ann was interested because she knew that something was missing from her life. She had never felt loved or cared for. The friend connected Ann to a Bible instructor who then began to study the Bible with her.

As the love of Jesus unfolded before her, Ann realized that all along, Someone had cared for her. There was Someone who actually loved her as she was, and she could finally let her guard down and trust Him to be there for her. She now knew that even in the worst of times, God had been with her. It was He who had brought her through her dark valleys, and it was He Who now made her feel secure and anchored. She found Elohim Ahavah, the God Who loves, and she never felt unloved again.

## Prayer:

*"There are so many times that I just need to feel loved and cared for. I need to have the assurance that I am loved unconditionally. I know that I have that in You, **Elohim Ahavah,** for You are the God of Love. Every day, You show me how much You love me. You made a plan of salvation for me so that I can live with You forever. Help me to recognize all the ways in which You demonstrate Your love for me. Thank You for loving me just as I am, but not leaving me that way, Elohim Ahavah."*

# – Chapter 15 –
# El Haggadol:
# Great God
## (ehl-hahg-ga-dohl)

*"For the LORD [YHWH] your God is God of gods and Lord of lords, the great God [El Haggadol], mighty and awesome, who shows no partiality nor takes a bribe." (Deuteronomy 10:17)*

I t was the end of forty years of wandering through the wilderness. All of the original adult travelers had died (except Moses, Joshua, and Caleb), and this was a new generation.

Moses, the 120-year-old leader of the Israelites, shared several admonishments in what became the book of Deuteronomy, the fifth and last book of the Pentateuch. [60]

*"And now, Israel, what does the LORD [YHWH] your God require of you, but to fear the LORD [YHWH] your God, to walk in all His ways and to love Him, to serve the LORD [YHWH] your God with all your heart and with all your soul, and to keep the commandments of the LORD [YHWH] and His statutes which I command you today for your good? Indeed heaven and the highest heavens belong to the LORD [YHWH] your God, also the earth with all that is in it." (Deuteronomy 10:12–14)*

It was important that the people obey God and not follow the example of their parents. It was critical that the Israelites, after having been in polytheistic Egypt and coming into a land where they would be surrounded by heathen nations, know Who the true God was: YHWH, El Haggadol, the Great God.

Moses had to remind the children of Israel that they had witnessed the wondrous acts of YHWH and that He would continue to be with them if they obeyed Him.

After Moses and Joshua died, the Israelites turned to the Canaanite gods, the Ashtoreths and Baal. Judges 2:12–13:

*"And they forsook the L*ORD *God of their fathers, who had brought them out of the land of Egypt; and they followed other gods, from among the gods of the people who were all around them, and they bowed down to them; and they provoked the L*ORD *[YHWH] to anger. They forsook the L*ORD *[YHWH] and served Baal and the Ashtoreths."*

The Israelites rejected YHWH and embraced the heathen deities, even after all He had done for them. They forgot how good He had been to them and began to look to other gods.

How often do we look to other gods, even when we know how good our God has been to us? We can look back on every trial and see that He brought us safely through it, and yet we sometimes forsake Him and look to our relationships, or careers, or money, or any other thing that we substitute for God. How heartbreaking it must be to Him when He has provided for us, and we ignore Him.

Israel broke their covenant with YHWH. Judges 2:11–23 and 3:1–6 portray an interesting story about how the people, after Joshua's death, reverted and became more corrupt than their fathers. They followed after other gods and worshiped them instead of the true God.

YHWH lifted His hand of protection from them, and the surrounding nations attacked them and prevailed. Then, the people would cry out to YHWH, so He would send judges to deliver them. Once delivered, they would fall right back into their old pattern of idolatry. This was such a vicious cycle, that God said:

*"Because this nation has transgressed My covenant which I commanded their fathers, and has not heeded My voice, I also will no longer drive out before them any of the nations which Joshua left when he died, so that through them I may test Israel, whether they will keep the ways of the L*ORD*, to walk in them as their fathers kept them, or not." (Judges 2:20–22)*

In Judges, the third chapter, we find what nations were left to test Israel. One of these nations was the Philistines, and they were a constant snare to the children of Israel.

One of my favorite stories and one that I must admit (although it is probably not intended to do so) brings a smile to my face is the story of YHWH and Dagon, the national god of the Philistines. In this story, the Philistines had gone to war with the children of Israel and had captured the ark of the covenant:

> "Then the Philistines took the ark of God and brought it from Ebenezer to Ashdod. When the Philistines took the ark of God, they brought it into the house of Dagon and set it by Dagon. And when the people of Ashdod arose early in the morning, there was Dagon, fallen on its face to the earth before the ark of the LORD [YHWH]. So they took Dagon and set it in its place again. And when they arose early the next morning, there was Dagon, fallen on its face to the ground before the ark of the LORD [YHWH]. The head of Dagon and both the palms of its hands were broken off on the threshold; only Dagon's torso was left of it." (1 Samuel 5:1–5)

I love this story. First of all, the Philistines thought that they were doing something big by taking the ark of the covenant into the house of their god, Dagon. They set it by Dagon, but the next morning, Dagon was in a worship position (face down) before the ark of the covenant. So they stood old Dagon back up, only to find the next morning that he was again in a prone position, but this time both his head and palms were broken off, indicating a powerless and mindless status before El Haggadol, the Great God.

I think that YHWH has a sense of humor and knows exactly how to get His points across to us frail humans.

> "For the LORD [YHWH] is great and greatly to be praised; He is also to be feared above all gods. For all the gods of the peoples are idols, but the LORD [YHWH] made the heavens. Honor and majesty are before Him; strength and gladness are in His place." (1Chronicles 16:25)

What YHWH did to Dagon frightened the Philistines, and they decided to send the ark of the covenant back to Israel where it rightfully belonged. The Philistines recognized that the God of Israel was all-powerful, and they were in awe of how He operated. They said:

> "The ark of the God of Israel must not remain with us, for His hand is harsh toward us and Dagon our god." (1 Samuel 5:7)

In spite of their idolatry, God still loved and cared for the Israelites. He also loved the Philistines, but they did not turn to Him. Even after all of this, they still claimed Dagon as their god.

There is a lesson for us in this as well. Even when we see the hand of God in our lives, sometimes we continue to cling to the idols that we have set up in God's place. We must remember that there is no god but God. He is YHWH, our El Haggadol.

There are no words that can adequately describe our awesome God. God, in all His greatness, loves you. It is mind-boggling to think that the Creator of the universe and everything that lives and breathes wants to be in an intimate relationship with His creatures. What is so special about us, that He would love us so? Perhaps we will have a chance to ask Him when we see Him face to face. In the meantime, we can marvel at the awesomeness of His mighty works and the innumerable ways in which He shows up in our lives.

YHWH is so amazing. He is indeed El Haggadol: the GREAT GOD!

*"You are great in counsel and mighty in work, for Your eyes are open to all the ways of the sons of men, to give everyone according to his ways and according to the fruit of his doings."* (Jeremiah 32:19)

Check out how He manifested Himself in Wisam's life:

## Wisam's Story

Wisam grew up in a very strong Muslim family in Nazareth, Israel. His father was the head of his tribe (family), which numbered more than two thousand one hundred men over the age of 21. This did not include women and children. From his youth, Wisam was educated and preparing to be an imam (a priest/pastor in the Islamic faith). He had to learn the Qur'an by heart, know Sharia law, and the Hadith (the writings of the Islamic prophet, Mohammed).

While training, Wisam was unfulfilled. Something was missing. He made the decision to leave the tribe, which was an insult to the family. Consequently, they removed his name from their tribal list. He was no longer considered a part of the tribe.

Wisam left the area and moved to Europe, where his sister was living. He discovered that his sister had become a Christian and was engaged to a Seventh-day Adventist pastor. His sister was a Christian? This infuriated Wisam. He contacted his estranged family with the news of his sister's Christianity and said that they needed to discuss the penalty for her new status.

Wisam went back to Israel and met with the council of elders and the young men from his tribe. He told them about his sister's conversion to Christianity. What he forgot to tell them, was that she was engaged to marry a Christian. In the Muslim faith, marrying a Christian is an immediate death sentence. Wisam feels that the Holy Spirit made him forget to share her engagement. The council told him to reach out to his sister and get her to repent. If she turned away from Christianity, all would be well.

Wisam went back to Europe and called his sister. He told her the decision of the tribe. They had a very challenging conversation that night. His sister boldly doubled down on her decision to remain a Christian, and asked him, "What does it profit me to gain the world, but lose my soul?" (See Mark 8:36). At the end of the conversation, they made an agreement: Wisam was to study the German language, and after one year, she would turn herself over to him. Wisam replied that if she did not honor her word about this, he would kill one Adventist every day until she did. He was not joking.

Through this journey, the Lord reached out to Wisam, and he converted to Christianity. He became a Seventh-day Adventist Christian. Instead of putting a stop to his sister's wedding, he helped her to get married.

After Wisam's baptism, he promised God that the first people who would hear about Jesus would be his tribe. So, he returned to Israel and went to the council of the elders and young men. The conversation went something like this:

Wisam's uncle, the imam, asked him, "How is your faith?"

Wisam said, "It is the best!"

Uncle: "Are you still praying five times a day? Are you still reading the Qur'an?

Wisam: "Before I answer this question, I have questions for all of you: "Who is the Creator?"

Council: "God is the Creator"

Wisam: "Who is the Healer?"

Council: "God is the Healer."

Wisam: "Who can raise the dead?"

Council: "God can raise the dead."

Wisam: "Then if God can do all of these things, why is Jesus mentioned in the Qur'an as doing exactly what God can do?"

Uncle: "Are you saying that Jesus is God?"

Wisam: "Uncle, I did not say it, but you proclaim it."

Wisam's uncle was very angry by now and commanded the young men to stone Wisam. They took him outside and stoned him. In that crowd were childhood friends of Wisam's whose countenances were now full of hatred for him. He would have been stoned to death, had his father not intervened by sending Wisam's brother into the crowd to hug Wisam. The crowd would stop the stoning because they did not want to injure anyone else. Wisam's mother dressed his wounds, and Wisam went back to the council. This time he took his Bible with him.

Wisam talked to the council for over three hours. He went from Genesis to the book of Revelation. At the end of the study, the imam said, "We have heard enough of this blasphemy. Kill him!" The young men grabbed Wisam and took him out to stone him again.

Wisam looked afar off and saw his mother weeping. She said to him, "Give up, son." Wisam replied, "Mother, I cannot give up Jesus. What would it profit me if I gain the world, but lose my soul?" His brother saved his life again by going to hug him, which stopped the stoning. They took Wisam to the hospital, and his wounds healed. He then left the country, labeled as an infidel. He knew that he could be killed by anyone, and they would not be punished for it.

Wisam returned to Europe and decided to work full time for the Lord. He earned a bachelor's degree in theology, and a master's degree. He began to travel the world teaching and preaching on how to reach out to Muslims.

In 2014, Wisam's mother called and invited Wisam and his family to come to Nazareth to take over the family business. She told him that all the men who had sought his life were now dead. Wisam, now married, said that they would come on certain conditions. He and his family would keep the Sabbath, they would practice their Christianity, and they would share Jesus with everyone who came into the company to do business. The mother agreed to all these conditions without hesitation. She even promised that the family would sign a statement of protection for Wisam, declaring him to be under their care while running the business.

In 2015, Wisam was invited to be in charge of the Arab outreach work. In that area there were seven million Arabs. Wisam is the director of the Life and Hope Center in Nazareth and Jerusalem. He also pastors two English-speaking churches. His ministry is bearing fruit: an entire Baptist church began studying with Wisam, and now attends his church on Sabbath.

Wisam says that Jesus has kept all His promises to him. The greatest promise being that He will fill us with His Holy Spirit. Do we trust Him? If we have faith, it means that we do not have fear. We can trust in YHWH, the El Haggadol. He will do great things in your life. Just try Him and see.

## Prayer:

*"Dear Lord, You are **El Haggadol, the Great God.** As I look at the world around me, and I see the wonders of Your creative power, I am amazed. But what astounds me the most is Your love for me. You continue to rescue me from the gods of this world, and even from physical danger. I can trust You because You are trustworthy. No other god compares to You. Please remove any 'god' in my life, other than You. For You and You alone are God. You are indeed, El Haggadol: the Great God."*

"Praise the LORD!
Praise the LORD from the heavens;
Praise Him in the heights!
Praise Him, all His angels;
Praise Him, all His hosts!
Praise Him, sun and moon;
Praise Him, all you stars of light!
Praise Him, you heavens of heavens,
And you waters above the heavens!
Let them praise the name of the LORD,
For He commanded and they were created.
He also established them forever and ever;
He made a decree which
shall not pass away."

–Psalm 148:1-6

# – Chapter 16 –

# YHWH Shammah:
# The Lord Is There

## (Alternate Name: Adonai Shammah)
## (a-do-nai shahm-mah)

*"All the way around shall be eighteen thousand cubits;
and the name of the city from that day shall be: THE
LORD [YHWH] IS THERE." (Ezekiel 48:35)*

The prophet Ezekiel's name in Hebrew was, "Yeheze' l," which means, "God Strengthens," or, "Strengthened by God."[61] Here was another case in which a name had significance in the individual's life, for Ezekiel needed strength to deal with the assignments and tasks of his ministry.

Ezekiel lived during the painful time of the Babylonian captivity of Judah. It was a situation that Israel had brought upon itself by perpetually disregarding God's laws and taking on the pagan customs and worship practices of the neighboring kingdoms. It had gotten to a place where they were even sacrificing their children in their worship of other gods. YHWH had given them multiple chances to repent and to turn back to Him, but they would not listen.

Now, before you shake your head at their disobedience, what about yours? How many times have you ignored the promptings of the Holy Spirit and done your own thing? I am certainly guilty of that from time to time. How many idols do we have in our own lives that need to be discarded and replaced by a focus on and commitment to God? Before we judge anyone else, we need to examine ourselves.

Despite the judgment that Israel faced, YHWH promised restoration. The children of Israel would be restored to their homeland after seventy years of captivity. The temple that was torn down during the Babylonian invasion would be rebuilt, and God would dwell with His people once again. The city would be called "YHWH Shammah: The Lord is there."

There is only one place in the Bible where YHWH Shammah occurs, and that is Ezekiel 48:35. It is the very last verse in the book of Ezekiel. In that text, the name YHWH Shammah is given to the city of

Jerusalem. This is also the last name and title of God revealed to His Old Testament prophets.[62]

The text teaches that the presence of YHWH, the "Self-Existent One," the One whose name denotes a God who is ever revealing Himself, is ever-present. The word "Shammah" is derived from its root, "sham," which is translated as "there."[63] In other words, God is there.

Just as God was sending a message of hope and restoration to His people, so it is with us as individuals. When we have moved away from God, when we have placed idols in the position of our hearts that only God should occupy, when we have strayed away and see no way forward, God can restore us. The same message that He sent to Israel, He gives to us today:

> "For I will take you from among the nations, gather you out of all countries, and bring you into your own land. Then I will sprinkle clean water on you, and you shall be clean; I will cleanse you from all your filthiness and from your idols. I will give you a new heart and put a new spirit within you; I will take the heart of stone out of your flesh and give you a heart of flesh." (Ezekiel 36:24–26)

Wherever you are, whatever state that you find yourself in, God will meet you where you are, and bring you to Him. There is nothing that you may have done that is too bad or out of reach of His forgiveness.

It is so comforting to know that our God is always there with us, no matter the challenge. There is no situation in our lives of which God is unaware. Wherever you are, He is there. YHWH Shammah has proven that to Jaime many times over.

## Jaime's Story

Jaime was born in Colombia and brought up in a very secular environment. His father was an alcoholic and wanted Jaime to be like him. He was very proud that Jaime was drinking at nine years of age and bragged about it to his friends.

As Jaime got older, he was drawn into gangs, with all the drinking and violence that goes along with it. He was in and out of juvenile detention centers, and by the time he was sixteen, he felt that he had had enough of that life. He decided to leave Colombia and go to the United States.

Here in the states, Jaime worked but developed relationships with young people who were all involved in the drug world. After two years of trying to stay outside of that world, Jaime found himself drawn into it. His first paid assignment was to smuggle money from the United States into Colombia. Then, he was offered the job of killing some high-level drug dealers. He refused that job but decided to set up his own drug distribution network.

Jaime built a chain of distribution from Texas to New York, Miami, Dallas, and Colombia. In fact, at his peak in that world, Jaime was Dallas's #1 drug dealer. Then, one day, things changed. He was arrested. While he was in jail, he made a decision. He thought, "As soon as I get out, I'm going to shut down everything and never do this again. It is just not worth it." That is just what he did. Only one week later, Jaime was released on a technicality, and he totally left the drug world. He became a car salesman and was successful at it.

One night, he went over to his boss's house where they were drinking. Jaime left and headed home drunk. He never made it back. He fell asleep and slammed into a tree and was knocked unconscious.

The next morning, a policeman approached his car, told him to roll down the window, and asked for his identification. Jaime obliged him and sat in his vehicle while the policeman returned to his. Jaime waited for several minutes. Then, two, four, six, eight, ten police cars came and surrounded his.

"What is happening?" Jaime wondered. The policeman came back to his car and said, "We have been looking for you for about a year now. There is a warrant for your arrest." Jaime told himself that there must have been some mistake. What he did not know was that after he was incarcerated, they had reopened his case. He was now in serious trouble. Jaime was arrested that day and sent to jail, awaiting extradition from Miami (where he lived at the time) to Texas.

Previously, when anyone tried to talk to Jaime about the Lord, he was not interested. He had absolutely no interest in hearing about God. This time, however, while incarcerated, he found a Bible in Spanish and began to read it. He could not understand any of it. Although he could not understand it, he continued to read it.

One night, while sleeping, by his own words he recalls, "something strong came to me." It was a feeling of joy and peace like he had never had. He knelt and began to pray. He opened his heart to the Lord. This went on until daylight. That next day, Jaime read his Bible, and it was as though a light switch had gone on. He understood what he was reading. He learned about the beautiful plan of salvation and found that if he confessed his sins and came repentantly to the Lord, He would forgive him and give him eternal life.

Jaime was so excited about this that he began to share this good news with other inmates and his family. He talked about Jesus to anyone who would listen. He now had hope and strength from the Word of God. What a blessing.

Jaime was extradited to Texas via Oklahoma. On the day that he was to leave Miami to go to Oklahoma, Jaime had his Bible in his hand, preparing to leave the prison. The guard told him that he was not allowed to remove that Bible and take it with him. To Jaime, it was like taking off his arm. What would he do without it? It was his lifeline. He practically begged the guard to let him take the book, but the guard flatly denied every plea. Reluctantly, Jaime left his Bible there.

It was late at night when he arrived at the facility in Oklahoma. Lights were out in the surrounding cells. No one was in the corridors as he was escorted to his cell. The correction officer secured Jaime in his cell and left. While looking the cell over, he looked up, and a black man was standing outside his cell. This was strange because there had been no other person in the hallway except the guard that had escorted him to his cell.

It was very late, and the inmates in the surrounding areas were asleep. The man asked Jaime, "Hey, would you like to have a Spanish Bible?" Jaime could not believe it. He gratefully reached through the bars and took the Bible. He looked at it, and when he looked up to thank the man, he had disappeared. Jaime believes that this was an angel. What a miracle.

Jaime was moved from floor to floor in the Oklahoma facility and shared Jesus with the other inmates. One particular inmate was very mean looking. He cursed Jaime when he met him and told him that he had killed twenty-three people, some of whom had been inmates there at that prison. Jaime said a silent prayer, and they began a conversation in which Jaime shared the plan of salvation with the inmate. The man started to cry. He opened his heart and accepted Jesus Christ as his Savior. A visible change took place in his countenance. He was a redeemed man. He now loved Jesus.

Jaime's sentence was supposed to be thirty-nine years in prison, but his attorney got him out. Jaime knows that it was his Divine Attorney, his Savior, his YHWH Shammah, Who was right there and delivered him. YHWH Shammah was always there with Jaime. When Jaime was in the gangs, He was there. When Jaime went to prison, He was there. When Jaime needed a Spanish Bible, YHWH Shammah was there. He is always there no matter what our life situation may be.

## *Prayer:*

*"Dear **Adonai Shammah,** my Lord Who is always there, it is a comfort to know that you are in the midst of my life at every juncture. There are strongholds in my life. I know that You know what they are and how to be delivered from them. I need You to step into my situation. (Share with God whatever that situation is). You are my strength and my defense. I cannot make it without You. I know that You are with me right now, although I may not see You. Thank You for being with me every second. You are the God Who Is Always There."*

"Praise the Lord!
Praise the name of the Lord;
Praise *Him*, O you servants of the Lord!"
−Psalm 135:1, 3

# Conclusion

This book is only a tip of the iceberg. There are at least one hundred titles for our great God, and none of them can completely or adequately describe the glory that is His. I just pray that the titles in this book have given you a closer look at His character and impress you with the great love that He has for you. If it has drawn you closer to Him, then, "Mission accomplished."

Take time to talk with Him, using these titles in your prayers. I guarantee that it will enrich your prayer life and deepen your connection to the Father and the Savior.

If you would like to commit or recommit your life to Jesus Christ, please repeat this prayer aloud: "Dear Lord Jesus, I know that I am a sinner, and I ask for Your forgiveness. I believe You died for my sins and rose from the dead. Please turn me from my sins as I invite You to come into my heart and life. I want to trust and follow You as my Lord and Savior."

If you are accepting Jesus for the first time, know that all of heaven is celebrating your acceptance of Jesus (Yeshua) as your Lord and Savior. This is the best decision that you could ever make.

To grow spiritually, you must study God's Word and pray to Him daily. On the last inner page of this book, you will find information about 3ABN, a 24/7 Christian television network dedicated to spreading the good news of Jesus Christ to the world. Tune in to 3ABN (parent network), or the 3ABN urban network, Dare to Dream (d2dnetwork. tv), or any of the 3ABN networks on television and radio. You will be blessed!

"Your name, O LORD, *endures* forever,
Your fame, O LORD, throughout all generations."
—Psalm 135:13

# Acknowledgments

There are so many people who have poured into this book. I am so very grateful to the contributors who shared their testimonies: Chris Hudson, Vala Ullberg, Dwight Hall, Magna Porterfield, Samuel Jacobson, Lotolua Iolua, Marc Lewis, Michael Carducci, Lionel Martell, Philip Ammons, Chris Shelton, Audrey Maher, Bruce Fjarli, Wendell Allen, "Ann," Wisam Ali, and Jaime Espinal. All of you were so kind and willing to tell of God's goodness in your lives. Thank you.

To Dr. Roy Gane, Professor of Hebrew Bible and Ancient Near Eastern Languages at Andrews Theological Seminary: How can I express my appreciation for the value of your insights? You helped me with the pronunciation of the Hebrew transliterations, and straightened me out on the YHWH issue, for which I am eternally grateful. Thank you for your time and expertise. You are a blessing.

Thanks to my friend, Kenny Karen, who took the time to help me with my Hebrew pronunciations and encouraged me in this journey.

This book could not have been written without the support of my precious family. To my dear husband, Danny: I love you, Honey. Thank you so much for your input and encouragement in this project. To my beloved children (biological and bonus kids): Marc (my firstborn who so graciously allowed me to share his journey in this book), and Jason (my "baby boy"who is always a great source of encouragement). Then there are my "bonus babies": Trinity, Melody and Greg, Valdez, Raymond, Toya, Tammy, Lisa, and Rhonda. I love you, along with my grandchildren, cousins, nieces, nephews, "sister-friends," and "brother-friends." You are all so precious to me. Thanks for always being there. Also, to my 3ABN Family: it is a privilege and a pleasure to serve with you in ministry. I love you all.

Thanks to my cousin Brian Thomas, who took the time to read and critique the first few chapters. Your constructive criticism caused me to re-evaluate and re-work all the chapters. It lengthened the process but yielded a much better end result. I praise the Lord for that and am grateful for your candor.

During the process of writing *Glimpses of His Glory*, I had hip surgery. My sister, Dr. Denise Robinson; my niece, Michelle Martell; dear friends, Ladye Love Smith, Jason and Francine Bergman, Greg and Jill Morikone; and precious in-laws, Kenny and Chris Shelton, came to Kentucky to be with me and encourage me. Thanks to Jackie Battle-Price, Gail Bennett, Pat Martell, Denise Gaynor, and all the 3ABN viewers who called and texted me during that time. I love you guys.

Shelley Quinn texted and encouraged me regularly, as she, herself, was recuperating from surgery. And then, once I completed this manuscript, she gave me some great suggestions. Thanks, dear "sis" Shelley.

Special thanks to my "Little Sis," Jill Morikone, who took the time out of her overflowing schedule to read and critique the manuscript. She reminded me of how to properly use commas and quotation marks. LOL!

Thanks to Ricky Carter, who designed the cover. You have great talent and a beautiful spirit.

Special thanks to Dwight Hall and the Remnant Publications team. Dwight, you are a blessing. Also, thank you for sharing your testimony in this book. I know that it will bless others immensely. Special thanks also to my editor, Ruth Stewart. Your suggestions were right on target!

Most importantly, I need to acknowledge the Great God of the Universe, YHWH. There are no words that adequately describe You. How I thank You for laying it on my heart to write this book. What a privilege and an honor to share with others just a glimpse of Your glory. Thank You from the bottom of my heart.

# Appendix

n the Hebrew Old Testament (or Tanakh), YHWH is God's most common designation, occurring over 6,000 times. It is composed of four Hebrew letters, which in English sound like Yod, Hey, Waw or Vav, and Hey. There were 22 letters in the original Hebrew alphabet, all of which represented consonants, with no vowels. Some of the consonants, such as Yod, Waw/Vav, and Hey, additionally came to be used as "vowel letters" to facilitate reading by indicating long vowel sounds. But the four letters in YHWH are all used as consonants.

Groups of Jewish scribe-scholars, called "Masoretes," meaning "Traditionalists," worked between the A.D. sixth and tenth centuries to preserve the Hebrew Bible, and they introduced a vowel notation system into the text.

However, the vowels in the pronunciation of the sacred name YHWH had been lost after the temple in Jerusalem was destroyed by the Romans in A.D. 70. So, the Masoretes used the vowels in the Hebrew word Adonai, "my Lord," which is a title of God in the Bible. They added these vowels to the four consonants YHWH, so that the word can be pronounced as Yehovah. By using vowels from another word, they insured that the Lord's personal name would not be taken in vain.

Jews commonly add an additional level of respect by reading Yehovah as Adonai or simply has-hem, "The Name." However, the Hebrew Bible has the words Adonai YHWH together hundreds of times (Genesis 15:2, 8, etc.), so reading YHWH as Adonai would result in repetition: Adonai Adonai. To avoid this problem, the Masoretes used the vowels in the word Elohim, "God," for YHWH in this combination, and Jews read it as Elohim. So, the combination sounds like Adonai Elohim.

Jehovah, the Masoretic form of YHWH, was written as Jehovah in the King James Version, under the influence of German, in which "j" is pronounced as "y". However, English versions usually translate YHWH as "the Lord," as if the Hebrew word were Adonai, following the lead of the ancient Greek Septuagint translation of the Old Testament, which rendered YHWH as kurios, "the Lord."

Yahweh is the pronunciation of YHWH that is most often used by Hebrew scholars, based on linguistic reconstruction (compare, for example, the shortened Hebrew form of the name that the Masoretes vocalized as Yah in Exodus 15:2; Psalm 118:14; Isaiah 12:2). But this may not be the original pronunciation because our knowledge of the vowels is uncertain. We can conclude that because the ancient Hebrew biblical text did not use any vowel markings, the actual pronunciation of the Sacred Name YHWH is simply not known.

# Endnotes

1   Genesis 1:1 is the very first verse in the Bible. It is here that we are introduced to Elohim as being the Creator of the universe.

2   Andrew Jukes, "The Names of God: Discovering God as He Desires to be Known" (Grand Rapids: Kregel Publications, 1967), p. 17.

3   Jukes, p. 18

4   Parkhurst's *Hebrew Lexicon*, alluded to by Andrew Jukes, p.19.

5   Jukes, p. 25.

6   According to biblestudytools.com, "Goel is the participle of the Hebrew word," gal'al ("to deliver', to redeem").

7   Job 1:12. Read Job 1 to see the dialogue between YHWH and Satan.

8   *Remnant Study Bible*, Commentary on the book of Ruth, Remnant Publications, 2009, NKJV.

9   For a more in-depth look into the concept of "kinsman redeemer," read Leviticus 25:47–49.

10  *Remnant Study Bible*, Commentary on the book of Ruth, Remnant Publications, 2009, NKJV.

11  Ibid.

12  Ibid.

13  Ibid.

14  Ibid.

15  Nathan Stone, *Names of God*, (Chicago: Moody Publishers, 2010 edition), p. 49.

16  Ibid.

17  Ibid.

18   Jukes, p. 66.

19   Ibid., p. 68.

20   Ibid., p. 63.

21   Ibid., p. 64.

22   Jukes, p. 69, referencing Acts 20:28.

23   Ibid., referencing Acts 2:17, 33.

24   Ibid., referencing John 7:37.

25   Ibid., referencing Psalm 81:10.

26   Ibid., p. 69.

27   Stone, p. 54.

28   Stone, p. 60.

29   https://biblestudytools.org. Tsur means "Rock" and is a title for God

30   https://hebrew-streams.org (Shem Yeshua Mashiach).

31   https://hebrew-streams.org. (Shem Yeshua Mashiach).

32   https://hebrew-streams.org. (Shem Yeshua Mashiach).

33   Ibid.

34   https://bible.org/illustration/be-set-apart-holy-use.

35   Ibid.

36   Ellen White, *Education*, p. 250.

37   Ellen White, *Acts of the Apostles*, p. 560.

38   "Binky" is a nickname for my sister, Gloria. Binky spent years away from the Lord (like I did), but returned to Him a few years before she died in 2009. Praise the Lord, once again, El HaNe'eman faithfully honored the prayers of my parents and grandmothers. Binky died in the Lord, and is peacefully sleeping until the Resurrection. Praise God.

39   Jeremiah 23:2.

40   Jeremiah 23:5.

41   Jeremiah 23:6.

42   *The Life Application Study Bible*, Tyndale House Publishers, Inc., 1996.

43   www.ellenwhitedefend.com/articles-Comp/righteousness_by_faith.htm.

44  You can find the story of King Ahaz in 2 Samuel 16, and 2 Chronicles 28.

45  https://www.biblestudytools.com/commentaries/treasury-of-david/psalms-24-7.html

46  Exodus 7–12 shares the saga of the 10 plagues placed by God upon Egypt.

47  Commentary in God's Word Translation, p. 100: "Yahweh Ropheka".

48  NEWSTART is the acronym for God's eight laws of health.

49  https://en.wikipedia.org/wiki/Salvation_in_Christianity.

50  Sylvanus Stall, *With the Children on Sundays*, "The Feast of Tabernacles".

51  Genesis 14:15–16.

52  Jukes, p. 87.

53  Ibid.

54  Ibid., p. 88.

55  https://livingtruth.ca/blogs/devotionals/babylon-s-resolve.

56  Ibid.

57  Daniel 4:10–26.

58  https://www.britannica.com/biography/Nebuchadnezzar-II.

59  https://www.britannica.com/biography/Nebuchadnezzar-II#ref98254.

60  The Pentateuch are the first five books of the Bible that were written by Moses.

61  *The Remnant Study Bible*, Commentary on the Book of Ezekiel, Remnant Publications, Inc., 2009.

62  www.myredeemerlives.com/namesofgod/yhwh-shammah.pdf.

63  https://www.blueletterbible.org/study/misc/name_god.cfm.

# 3ABN: The Mending Broken People Network
## Ways to watch & listen to 3ABN

**Local TV** – Check the cable and television stations in your local area for 3ABN

**DISH** – Channel 9393*, visit **dish.com**
*available upon request*

**Verizon FiOS** – Channel 291, visit **buyverizon.com**

**Apple TV** – Download the **mySDAtv app** on the Apple TV app store

**Amazon Fire TV** – Stream 3ABN directly to your TV

**YouTube** – Over 2,400 videos on-demand at **3ABNVideos**

**Roku.com** – Stream 3ABN directly to your TV

**3ABN app** – (iPhone, iPad, Android) download the **3ABN app**

**Live 24/7 Streaming** – Through our website **3ABN.tv** or on our **Truli.com** 3ABN page

**Radio** – Available on over 300 radio stations around the world **3ABNRadio.org**

## 3ABN
### Three Angels Broadcasting Network

*Info: 618.627.4651 or visit 3ABN.tv*